I0192499

THE LONGEST SHADOW

© Copyright 2015- Mark A. Wyatt

All rights reserved. Permission is granted to copy or reprint portions for any noncommercial use, except they may not be posted online without permission.

Wyatt House books may be ordered through booksellers or by contacting:

WYATT HOUSE PUBLISHING
399 Lakeview Dr. W.
Mobile, Alabama 36695
www.wyattpublishing.com
editor@wyattpublishing.com

Because of the dynamic nature of the Internet, any web address or links contained in this book may have changed since publication and may no longer be valid.

Cover design by: Mark Wyatt

ISBN 13: 978-0-9915798-3-9

Printed in the United States of America

THE LONGEST SHADOW

—— THE LIFE AND LEGACY OF ——

HOWARD L. MISKELLY

BY MARK WYATT

Wyatt House Publishing
Mobile, Alabama

This book is dedicated to my faithful and loving Parents-in-law, Milton and Ann Varner.

They are part of the reason why their generation is called the greatest one.

Author's Introduction
by Mark A. Wyatt

I watched from the lobby of the hotel as Chip Miskelly drove up, with his father, Howard Miskelly in the front passenger seat and his mother, Ann, behind Howard. We were about to have dinner before beginning our interviews for this book. We drove to a down-home country cooking restaurant in West Point, Mississippi, exited the car, and proceeded to go inside. At least most of us did. On our way in, we nodded and said *hello* to a young couple on their way out. As we approached our table, I noticed that Howard wasn't with us. He had stopped outside to talk to the young couple. They were new in town, he found out, recent graduates of Mississippi State, and were now living and working in West Point. Howard also found out, in short order but without being the least bit offensive, that they had not found a church to attend yet.

It must be understood, though, that it was about ten or fifteen minutes later when I heard all of this, because that's how long Howard stood outside talking. By the time he came to the table, Chip, Ann, and I had ordered (Ann ordered for Howard), finished our salads, and the food was on its way. But waiting for Howard was time well spent. Watching him through the glass door, talking so warmly to strangers some sixty years his junior, showed me more about him in that fifteen minutes than I would learn over the next few months of conversation.

What I learned was that Howard Miskelly loves people. All of them. He also loves his life, and it shows. He has been incredibly successful, and he is honored constantly and recognized widely, but, well and truly, none of that matters to him. He just loves waking up in the morning and finding out what the day holds. And when you can do that at 89 years of age, you're doing something right.

Writing a book is a team effort. As always, the patience and encouragement of my wife and children have kept my nose above water long enough to get back to shore. So, to Mary Ann, Samuel and his wonderful new wife Sydney, Sarah, Nathaniel, and Autumn, thank you for helping me get another one out.

I owe a great debt of thanks to Chip Miskelly for putting this work into action, as well as his siblings, for their stories; and to Howard and Meme for their time, their kindness, their openness, and their spare bedroom. I am honored to have written the life story of this man, and if it were many thousands of words longer, I still could not say enough to describe him to you. But, hopefully, in the words that are here, your life will be made richer by knowing Howard Miskelly just a little bit more. Mine certainly has been.

Oh, and did I tell you, that young couple at the restaurant did, in fact, come to visit Howard's church the next Sunday. Because, really, how can you say "no" to Howard?

Mark A. Wyatt, Ph.D.
January, 2015
Mobile, Alabama

Foreword
by Jackie Sherrill

The first time I met Mr. Howard Miskelly was at the "M" Club meeting at Mississippi State University in December of 1990. It was the announcement of my new position as the head football coach at MSU and Mr. Miskelly walked up and introduced himself:" I am Howard Miskelly and I'm very excited that you are our new football coach." I knew he must be a great friend to MSU, but little did I know at that time what a great friend he would become to me.

There's no shortage of folks who want to be involved in a university football program but a man like Mr. Miskelly is a rare gift. From our first conversation I knew he was a man of intelligence, integrity and deep faith. He has the ability to listen without judging, advise without blaming and to encourage without demeaning. It's not difficult to see how he built his furniture store into the booming success it is and this book may well serve as a valuable tutorial for anyone hoping to follow suit. There's worthwhile information in this book that's as pertinent today as the day Howard Miskelly first put it to use and not just information about running a successful business. There are lessons about life in these pages and I think that may be the genius behind this book.

Thank you, Mr Miskelly, for the friendship and the opportunity to be a part of your story.

Jackie Sherrill
Head Football Coach
Mississippi State University, 1991-2003

Foreword
by Dr. Fred H. Wolfe

It is an honor to write a foreword for Howard Miskelly. A few years ago, I got to know Howard through his family, mainly his sons, Chip, Oscar, and Tommy. As I reflect on the life and legacy of Howard Miskelly, there is so much we can learn and be impacted by in his life.

Howard's genuine faith in Jesus Christ, his devotion to Christ and His Word, the Bible, has permeated every area of his life. Howard has truly followed Christ in all he has done. He has a magnetic personality, a gift from God, that draws people to him. When Howard is present, it influences everyone in the room.

Howard has been a very successful and wise businessman, building a business with honesty, integrity, and love for people, always treating them with dignity and respect.

Howard's devotion to his wife and children are a joy to behold. You can see in Ann's face how Howard treats her with love and kindness. His daughters, Pam and Marty, show with their lives the benefits of being raised by a loving father. His sons, Chip, Oscar, and Tommy, are a great legacy. He has instilled in all of them the same faith, values, and work ethic that he has lived out. The success of Miskelly Furniture bears the mark of Howard Miskelly. Howard has deeply loved his Lord, his family, his church, and his country.

This book is a must-read for all of us because it will inspire us, instruct us, and show us by example how to live a life pleasing to God. Your life will be blessed, and you will be stronger and wiser as a result of having read the biography of this amazing man.

Howard Miskelly has already left a great legacy- a mark that cannot be erased. He has been a blessing to my life. Read and be blessed by his life as well!

Dr. Fred H. Wolfe
Pastor Emeritus, Cottage Hill Baptist Church, Mobile, AL
Pastor for a Season, Crossgates Baptist Church, Brandon, MS
Present Pastor, Luke 4:18 Fellowship, Mobile, AL

"A man's heart plans his way,
but the Lord determines his steps."

-*Proverbs 16:9*

From the desk of Bob Tyler, former head coach of Mississippi State University, 1973-1978:

October 26, 2014

Dear Howard:

CONGRATULATIONS on your football team's achievement of the Number One position in the National Ranking. I thought of you the very moment I heard about the Bulldogs' Number One ranking.

When I was coaching in Okolona, I looked forward to coming to your store to talk about football and have fun. Later, as your coach at Mississippi State University, I was eager to travel to your area and see you. You have always been a good friend.

Everywhere I coached, both high school and college, there were always a few unique, special and extremely loyal men who worked closely with us to increase our team's chances of winning, and I have traditionally called those men *Long Shadows*. I applied that title to these men because their faces and personalities are imprinted in my memory, but primarily, because their way of thinking about winning and achieving, like rare shadows, will forever fall across my mind influencing my way of thinking. You are the best of the best of all of those Long Shadows!

Knowing you has been a blessing for me. I wish all the best wishes for you and Ann and your fine family. I hope to visit with you again in the near future.

I am glad your Bulldogs are winning big.

Sincerely,
Bob Tyler

PROLOGUE

Capitol Building
Jackson, Mississippi
January 17, 2014

Voices echoed and dress shoes clacked on the marble floor under the 180-foot high dome inside Mississippi's grand Capitol Building in Jackson, warm and protected against a cold January wind outside. Reporters checked their notes while cameramen set up lights on stands. The subject of their focus stood quietly to the side, knowing why they were there, but wondering why all these people would make such a fuss over him. Still, Howard L. Miskelly was proud to be there. He waited patiently, his white hair contrasted with a dark suit and modest tie, his six foot-two inch frame just slightly bent from the weight of eighty-eight years. When he was instructed, Howard Miskelly took his place between a decorated Air Force major general, a congressman, and the Governor of his state.

Governor Dewey "Phil" Bryant, after being introduced, stepped to a podium bearing the great seal of the state of Mississippi, and addressed the assembled crowd by directing his first remarks to Howard's wife of sixty-six years, Ann. "Mrs. Miskelly," he began, "I know it is challenging sometimes when you hear great things said about your husband. But I know that you will agree with all of us, that Howard Miskelly has made a difference in this world, and in this state, and in the many lives that he has touched. What a wonderful family you have. I know that even as proud as we are of the wonderful, heroic acts of Mr. Miskelly, the greatest thing that he has done in his lifetime, is marry you and have these wonderful children."

"True," says Howard Miskelly in the background, as he nods in agreement.

After referring to Howard's enlistment in the Army as a young man, Governor Bryant continued. "His division," he said, "fought in Belgium, Holland, and Germany, where he was involved in intense combat, something few of us know in this world. It was during that fighting that he earned the Combat Infantry Badge, and ultimately, as we complete today, the awarding of the Bronze Star Medal.

"Now, this medal is awarded to persons while serving in any capacity in the United States Army after December the 7th, 1941, and we all remember that day. But that individual must distinguish himself or herself by heroic, meritorious actions in achievements or in service connected with military operations against an armed enemy and while engaged in a military operation involving conflict with the opposing armed forces. This is an award not given, but earned.

"Little did I know, until recently," the Governor continued, "that Mr. Miskelly was someone that we would call 'hero.' We use that term in our dedication in sincerity. Because you see, Howard Miskelly is one of the great generations that would have never told you he was a hero, that would never have thought of himself in that way. Like hundreds of thousands and millions of young men and women, he simply went to the call of his country, and he did so with honor and with valor. And it is our great joy today to help recognize him for that service.

"Mr. Miskelly, it is my great honor to know you, to be your friend, and now to be someone who recognizes the great and noble work that you have given to the United States of America. Thank you, sir."

Upon being called to the podium, Howard Miskelly faced Maj. Gen. Wayne Burkes, USAF (Ret.), and presented himself for the medal. Maj. Gen. Burkes pinned the Bronze Star on Howard's lapel, smiled, saluted him, and said, "Congratulations." Applause filled the rotunda as Howard turned, grasped the sides of the podium, and made remarks of his own. "I'd like to make about three points right quick," he began. "One is, you can't imagine how much it cost me to get them to make these nice remarks," he said, to respectful laughter. "Number two is, I didn't know I had this many friends." Then tears entered his eyes and voice as he choked out his next words. "And number three is, God bless you, and I love y'all!"

But it was after the award ceremony, as Howard Miskelly graciously made his way around the rotunda talking with reporters, that his deepest values were spoken. In those remarks, the ones that just flowed easily from his heart, Howard summed up his entire life. Cheryl Lasseter, from WLBT News, gave him the opening when she asked him if he had any advice for someone with ambition. "Just keep working on it," he said, "and don't leave the Lord out. I keep saying that, but if you want to be successful, you've got to include Him. Because it doesn't matter how much money you make, if you don't have that, you don't have anything."

And that is the core of Howard Miskelly's life. It is the one overarching value that has directed all of his decisions, from the time he was a barefoot boy on a dairy farm way out in Falkner, Mississippi.

CHAPTER 1
Mississippi Dirt

The little boy held his father's hand as he kicked the dirt clods in front of him on their way down the main street of Ripley. It was a sultry day in northern Mississsppi, which wasn't unusual for this time of year, and the boy's thin cotton shirt clung to his back and sides, damp with sweat. Ripley was certainly not a bustling metropolis, but it was the county seat of Tippah County. "Tippah" was the Indian word for "cut off," and even though Ripley was only 100 miles from Memphis, Tennessee, it did feel cut off from the world a bit, which was just how the residents liked it. Farms and vast open spaces made up the landscape, and the peace and quiet of it all was comforting.

Howard Miskelly was four years old when he walked

that street with his father in 1929, and though he wasn't sure why they had come the whole eight miles into town from Falkner, he was up for the adventure. Within a few minutes, Howard and his father stopped in front of a man sitting behind a barrel at the edge of the street. This barrel was where Uncle Simon Finger conducted his business.

Homer Miskelly stuck out his hand. "Good morning, Uncle Simon," he said, "how are you today?"

"Good morning, Homer," he said, taking the hand. "I'm just fine, thank you. And who's this strapping young buck you got with you? Can't be Howard. This'un here's almost grown!"

"Yessir, that's him alright. I keep feedin' him and he keeps growin'. Dang'dest thing."

"Well. What can I do for you, Homer?"

"I heard that doctor down in Falkner couldn't make his payments no more. I aim to borrow the money to buy his place."

"That is a fine, place, Homer, you're right to want it. How much do you need?"

"Twenty-five hundred dollars for the new house he just built and the 52 acres."

Uncle Simon opened a tattered leather satchel that looked older than he was, and pulled out a few sheets of paper. He slid a pencil from behind his ear, licked the tip of it, and began figuring. "Let's see," he said, "That'd come out to a payment of a hundred dollars a year for you. That sound about right for you?"

"Yessir," said Homer Miskelly, "that'll do just fine. I've already started getting the cows and mules that I need to make a go of it."

"I've no doubt of it, Homer, you're a fine man and a hard worker. Just sign right here." Uncle Simon spun the paper around on the barrelhead and pointed to a blank line he had drawn. Homer let go of Howard's hand, bent over slightly, and signed his name to the document. "Alright," said Uncle Simon, "I'll be right back." He took the document, got up from his cane back chair, and walked into a nearby building while pulling a key ring from his pocket and sorting through it. A few minutes later, he came out, walked over to the barrel, and counted out two thousand five hundred dollars on the top of it. "Cash on the barrelhead," he said. "Good luck to you, Homer," he said as he offered his hand. Homer shook Uncle Simon's hand, picked up the cash, and said, "Thank you, sir. I'll be faithful with your payments." He tousled Howard's hair. "With help like this by my side, how could I fail?"

Homer Miskelly's folks had come over from Ireland, which to most people, was evident from his last name. A few years earlier, Homer had met and married his pretty wife Wardie, whose family had come from England. That kind of "mixed marriage" might have been frowned upon in both of the old countries, but this was a land of opportunity, and Homer had seized his opportunity with Wardie. Wardie's father was a brilliant man, and in fact had started the Bank of Falkner, but Homer didn't want to borrow money from him for the farm. He didn't want anyone to think that he was getting special treatment. He needed to make it on his own.

They had a little girl first, Elva, then three years later, a boy. They named him Howard Lafayette Miskelly. Lafayette wasn't a family name, and it had no other special meaning to them. They just liked the sound of it. Howard would later joke that he was probably fifteen years old before he could spell it. With a wife, a daughter, and a son, Homer Miskelly knew that he had what was called a "rich man's family." And now, with a house and 52 acres, he felt that it was certainly true.

As time went on, young Howard Miskelly learned what it meant to run a farm. By the time he was nine years old, he was plowing. They had thirteen dairy cows that all had to be milked by hand, twice a day, every single day, whether the weather was steaming hot or below freezing. Rain, snow, sun, it didn't matter. The cows couldn't milk themselves. And Howard was out there, every day, without fail.

Howard learned early how to work the needle valve separator to separate out the cream. They would then sell the cream, take the skim milk, add shorts to it and feed it to the hogs. Then, in the spring, they would sell the hogs for fertilizer in time for spring planting. As Howard grew older, he was running the cream station on Saturdays, testing and weighing the cream. Only later did the Miskelly family venture into selling the actual milk.

In 1937, Homer and Wardie Miskelly and their children were enjoying their life on the farm. Farm life in the country also meant knowing, and being known by, your neighbors. Even though the "next door" neighbor might be a half mile away, it was your community, and part of life was taking care of each other.

Howard turned twelve that year, and one of his good friends, Cornelius Adams, lived down the road and around the curve. Cornelius lived with his mother and father, and they were one of a number of black families that made a decent living as sharecroppers on farms like the Miskellys'. That year, though, Cornelius' father died, and then his mother died about six months later. Usually, in a circumstance like that, one of the other black families would step up and take Cornelius in, but this time, no one came for him. So, Cornelius was slated to be taken to the poor house in Ripley. The poor house was just that, a place that would give him just enough food to keep from starving to death, and some sort of shelter. It was not a family, nor could it be. Cornelius was about to be on his own.

"We'll not have it," said Homer Miskelly to his wife

when he heard. "He ain't going to live there. He's going to live here." And so it was that Cornelius Adams came to live with the Miskellys. Cornelius and Howard were the same age and the same size, and they both gained a brother. They fought like brothers, rode bulls and horses together, and worked on the farm together. Cornelius still had to go to school and church in the black area of Ball Hill, but he lived with a white family who was glad to have him. There was never any backlash from anyone in the community. Everyone had loved Cornelius' mother and daddy, and they were happy that he was happy.

When Howard was drafted in 1943, Cornelius stayed. While Howard was gone, Cornelius fell in love and married, and Homer built them a house on the farm. Cornelius lived with them for forty years in all. Homer Miskelly made Cornelius save a little money every year, and eventually he had enough to buy his own farm with a house and 50 acres, and he and his wife moved there.

Howard had another close friend growing up in Falkner, a neighbor named Curtis Richardson. Curtis lived next door, although "next door" was relative when you lived in the country. Curtis's family was wealthy, at a time when money was nowhere to be had for most people. "Wealthy" was also a relative term in the 1930's, but Mr. Richardson was gainfully employed as a mailman. He had two routes, Route 1 and Route 2, and though he worked long hours, his job netted him about $400-$500 per month. This was the same time period in which Howard's daddy, Homer, might work at the cotton gin for ten hours to earn a one dollar bill. Curtis Richardson's father made more than ten times that much.

The Richardsons, then, had the ability to travel whenever they wanted to. They were good people, and they were good to Howard. They never acted like they were better than anyone else, and they took care to prove it. Wherever they went, they took Howard with them. Most young boys couldn't dream of riding a flatbed truck a hundred miles away for vacation, but Howard not only dreamed it, he lived it with the Richardsons.

When Curtis and Howard were in high school, they would make money by taking part of Mr. Richardson's mail route, Route 2. And, just like Mr. Richardson, they delivered it on horseback, for six to eight hours, rain or shine. Nothing was going to keep them from their appointed rounds.

Howard attended his family's Primitive Baptist Church when it was held on the 1st and 3rd Sundays of the month, but on the other Sundays, he went to the Methodist Church with Curtis and his family.

In the Miskelly household, faith in God was not only normal, it was essential. There was a constant recognition that a relationship with God was as necessary as rain on the crops and food for the cows. To that end, they were faithful members of a Primitive Baptist Church in their community, and Wardie Miskelly read the Bible to the whole family every night. She would read a chapter before bedtime to Homer, Elva, and Howard, even when they weren't listening.

When Howard was ten years old, his mother announced that they were changing churches. "Changing churches?" said Howard. "What for?"

"Well, son," said Wardie, "Primitive Baptists don't believe in foreign mission work, but in my reading of the Bible, I think God does. So, we're going to join the First Baptist Church in Falkner, because they believe in foreign missions, too."

Howard Miskelly lived a simple and wonderful life with his family on the farm, even when there was no money, because life didn't consist in the things that you owned, but in the people that you loved. What Howard didn't know was that soon he would find another one of those people the moment he laid eyes on a pretty girl named Ann Street.

CHAPTER 2
The Girl in the Pinafore Dress

Ann Street had quite a life in Ripley, Mississippi. She was the middle of three girls, all of them pretty, all of them popular. Ann's daddy, Oscar, was a lawyer, but he was also a brilliant entrepreneur. Before the Depression, Oscar and some friends had put in the light and water department, running power lines from the Mississippi-Tennessee border down to Ripley and beyond. They had also built an ice plant, and in the days before widespread refrigeration, an ice plant was booming business. They had each made a good bit of money, and though Oscar had reinvested some and had loaned out more to help some young men go to college, the Street family still had plenty of money when, for most people, there was no money to be had.

It was because of their financial stability that the Street family became philanthropists when practically no one even knew there was a word for it. Her mother was a welfare department before anyone had thought of a welfare department. They had one of the few good cars around, so people were constantly asking Ann's mother for rides. She took them to the doctor, or to buy groceries, or to get to work. She was always willing to help. Once, she came home, took the shoes off Ann and her sisters' feet, turned around, went back out, and gave the shoes away to someone else. Of course the girls would get other shoes, but they always knew that whatever their family owned, it was likely to be given away to someone in need at any given time.

Business sense was not just a male attribute in this family, though. Ann's mother and grandmother also owned and operated the only movie theater in a 40-mile radius, called *The Dixie*. It was the Golden Age of Hollywood, and stars like Shirley Temple, Joan Crawford, Clark Gable, and Humphrey Bogart held moviegoers in thrall and gave them an escape from the miseries of everyday life. And on any Saturday in Ripley, the movie house was full. People would come in their wagons from all around. They would park their wagons on the square and spend the day buying groceries and going to the movies. For ten cents, starting at eleven in the morning, you could catch a double feature and all of the included serials.

Of course, not everyone had ten cents. Ann's grandmother was strict about not letting anyone in who did not have the price of admission. Ann's mother, though, held a different view. When children couldn't pay, as they walked away with long faces, she would catch their eyes and subtly jerk her head to a side door. They got to see the show. There, she would let them in without grandmother knowing. If they were black, they had to go upstairs with the other blacks, but that didn't matter. Almost always, though, these kids did not forget their benefactor, and they would show up later in the week to mow the lawn. Ann just figured it was like getting your grass cut for ten cents.

Every now and then, Ann's mother and grandmother would have to go to Memphis to pick up the new movies. Since Memphis was a hundred miles away, it became a whole day's adventure. Ann and her sisters and cousins would go along, where they would get dropped off at one end of a downtown street, and spend all day shopping. They would each get a dollar to spend, and by the time they made it to the opposite end of the street, they had spent their dollar, one dime at a time. From Lowenstein's, to jewelry stores, to five and dime stores, to Morrison's cafeteria, it was a thrilling time.

In their hometown of Ripley, children played in the

yard on swings, everyone skated, and neighbors were good to neighbors. There were lots of those neighbors, and it seemed that all of them were related in some way. Ann's younger sister had a wonderful playhouse and loved to play outdoors.

On Sunday afternoons, everyone would gather for Sunday dinner at grandmother's house up on the hill, but on the occasions that any of them played inside, nobody went upstairs in the old house. It was common knowledge among the children that there were ghosts up there.

The whole family attended these weekly Sunday dinners. Everyone, that is, except for Ann's father, Oscar. His mother-in-law had ten children, including some pretty wild boys, and he politely declined the standing invitation.

Every other weekend, 16-year-old Howard Miskelly was allowed to drive his father's 1937 Ford into Ripley. Howard had a girl there, Martha Rae. Howard and Martha Rae were dating, but not really dating. She was a year older than he was, and he liked her, but she was really more of a girl that was a friend, than a girlfriend. But, they did spend a lot of time together, and he called on her when he came to town.

One Sunday afternoon, Howard and Martha Rae were pulled up for curbside service at the local drugstore. The tray was on the window and they were waiting on their Coke floats when three girls came out of the store. Howard noticed one of them in particular.

"Hey, Martha Rae," he said.

"Yes?" she said.

"Who's that girl there in that pinafore dress?"

"Who, her?" said Martha Rae. "Oh, that's Ann Street. Her daddy's a lawyer and they own *The Dixie*."

"Hm," said Howard. "Ann Street."

Ann was only 14 years old then, but she had registered on Howard Miskelly's radar. A few months later, he went into Ruth Renfroe's café and used her phone to call the Street residence. "Hello, Ann," said Howard when she came to the phone. "This is Howard Miskelly," he said. "Do you know who I am?"

"Yes," said Ann, "I've seen you."

"Well," said Howard, "I want a date with you."

"That's very nice," she said, "but I'm not going out much."

"Well, can I come see you at your house some time?"

"I suppose," said Ann. "Call me again and we'll see."

About a week later, Howard called her again, and the front door of her home opened to him soon after.

Even after he started seeing Ann, though, he continued to spend time with Martha Rae, who lived just up the hill and across the street from Ann. One Saturday night, Howard walked out of Martha Rae's house at about ten o'clock, and found that his car was no longer parked outside of her house. It was just gone. He stepped into the street and looked both ways, searching for it. He walked over to the top of the hill, looked down, and there, parked in front of Ann's house, was his car. Ann and some of her friends had silently rolled it down there while Howard was visiting Martha Rae. It seemed she was staking her claim. Howard was not upset.

His car disappeared from in front of Martha Rae's house and appeared in front of Ann's at least two or three more times. Ann was definitely making her move. And as time went on, it became clear that Martha Rae was moving into the "more like a sister" zone while Ann was firmly laying hold of the coveted title of "girlfriend."

Howard was a good boy from a good family, so Ann's mother and daddy took to him fairly well. Oscar treated Howard as amiably as any other father would, looking at a 16-year-old boy dating his 14-year-old daughter. But, in the early 1940s, a daughter who was fourteen might reasonable only be two or three years away from being married.

Oscar and Annie Street were nice to Howard, as he was to them. Only once did Howard find himself in an awkward situation. During their courting season, Ann's family had a swing out on their front porch, as did many people. One evening, Howard was sitting on the swing, and Ann was sitting on his lap. Within just a few minutes, Oscar Street walked out of the front door, saw them, and stopped quickly. He went back in the house, and emerged moments later with a single chair. Oscar quietly walked over to the swing and put the chair down right by it. He never said a word. Then he continued on his way.

Howard could hardly swallow. The message was clear. Ann did not sit on Howard's lap on that swing again. At least not when Mr. Oscar was watching.

Oscar was gentle but firm, and the boys that dated his girls were more than a little intimidated by him. Ann told him once, "Daddy, all my boyfriends are scared of you!"

Oscar shrugged it off. "Aw," he said, "I knew that boy's daddy, and he wasn't scared of a rattlesnake. That boy ain't scared of me." Ann always suspected, though, that her daddy realized and relished his quiet power over all the potential suitors in Ripley, Mississippi.

CHAPTER 3
Over There

In April of 1943, on his eighteenth birthday, Howard Miskelly registered for the draft. World War II was in full swing, and it didn't take long for Uncle Sam to come knocking on Howard's door with a promise to see the world. He was soon drafted into the United States Army, 102nd Infantry Division, otherwise known as the Ozark Division.

The day before he left for the Army, an aunt brought him a very special gift. She gave him a small Bible, a New Testament bound in armor plating. "I want you to have this," she told him. "May it keep you from harm."

Howard took the Bible carefully, put it in his shirt pocket, and carried it every day for the next four years.

On September 15, 1942, at Camp Maxey, Texas, a long dormant Army Division was revived. The Ozark Division's creation was authorized at the end of World War I, but its organization had not been finished when the Armistice was signed in 1918. Mothballed and shelved away, the dust was blown off of it in an effort to increase America's fighting ground troops less than a year after the U.S. entered the European Theater. Under the command of Maj. Gen. John B. Anderson, the 102nd Division was reactivated and prepared to host the 15,000 men who would soon be joining its ranks.

It was called the Ozark Division after the hills of Arkansas and Missouri, whose men were supposed to have filled the original organization in the First World War. Instead, the Division took pride in the fact that it was actually made up of soldiers from every state in the Union. The largest number of troops came from Pennsylvania (1,579), and the least from Hawaii (4), with one soldier each hailing from Puerto Rico and the Panama Canal Zone, which was under United States authority.

According to the Infantry Journal, *With the 102nd Infantry Division Through Germany*, edited by Major Allan H. Mick:

> "The men who were to bring the Division to life did everything Americans do. They were clerks and grocers, section hands and lawyers,

millwrights and barbers, lumberjacks and teachers, as well as bookies and biologists, embalmers and seamen, chemists and trappers. They were toolmakers, musicians, turbine operators, farmers, welders, librarians, butchers, nurses, well drillers, cowhands, ranchers, and ministers. These men, with arms sore from inoculation and many with tags still on their uniforms, began to stream in to Camp Maxey in October. The infiltration continued throughout November and December until all 15,000 had arrived.

"At once they were formed into units and launched into intensive training, the purpose of which was not too clear to many of them at the time. Everyone realized, however, that arduous days lay ahead--days of effort, hardship, loneliness, and boredom. Less clearly they foresaw that this severity would be relieved by occasional pauses for recreation, by short visits at home, and above all by never-to-be-forgotten comradeship. Although the goal lay far ahead, its outlines could be faintly seen, and it was not without hope that the 102d launched into the serious business of forming an integrated fighting machine."[1]

Howard Miskelly would not join the 102nd until

they arrived in England, but the mettle of his fighting comrades would be formed and honed on the training grounds of Fort Maxey, Texas. There, the Division was involved in intense training, from constructing landmines to reconnaissance and intelligence skills. In November 1943, they were moved to Camp Swift near Austin. Soon, the commanders and staff began to anticipate the commencement of Preparation for Overseas Movement, or POM. On June 10, 1944, six days after D-Day, orders arrived to move to Fort Dix in North Carolina. Since Fort Dix was on the eastern seaboard, the logical guess was that they would be entering the European Theater.

On September 9, 1944, the Division was alerted that they would soon be boarding transports, and on September 11, they began boarding the ships moored at the Staten Island Base: "As midnight approached and New York's twinkling lights blinked out for the night the 102d Infantry Division waved goodbye to 'Miss Liberty.' By daylight on 12 September the six ships carrying the division--John Ericsson, Marine Wolf, Santa Paula, Sea Tiger, Bienville and the Marina--were proudly steaming in their appointed places. The convoy of forty-six vessels of all types was accompanied by a naval escort which seemed diminutive in contrast to their size. The 102d Division stood out for the open sea and France."[2]

Twelve days later, the Ozark Division arrived in the

war-torn Cherbourg Harbor. "One of the most profitable forms of training undertaken by the Division at this time," said the Infantry Journal, "was the clearing of mines and booby traps. In the vicinity of Area M there were still extensive German minefields which had formed part of the defenses of the Cherbourg Peninsula. They presented an opportunity for the perfecting of the technique of detecting and clearing these hidden engines of death and in disarming them and studying them. All of the hazards inherent to such an operation were present, except that of hostile fire. Ammunition and pioneer platoons, and the Reconnaissance Troop participated in this work which was a practical culmination of the comprehensive mine training they had received in the States. This 'finishing course' proved its value later when the units entered the lines and encountered many enemy minefields. The Ozarks then approached their mine-clearing task with confidence and accomplished them with minimal casualties."[3]

Howard spent his basic training at Camp Wolters, among the dry heat and scrub trees in Mineral Wells, Texas. He would go on to serve there until he was shipped out to England in the fall of 1944. It was October 4th when Howard joined the 102nd as a replacement. On October 22nd, the 406th Infantry, including the 19-year-old Howard Miskelly, boarded crowded boxcars for the three-day train trip to the front.

Howard had made friends with another young man who happened to be the son of a famous and powerful movie producer. The young man now found himself in the army, but he had no intention of getting killed on the front lines. Howard was not a small man, but his new friend wore a size 15 AAA shoe. On the train ride to the front, the producer's son threw his oversized shoes out of the train window and into a river, knowing full well that it might very well take until the end of the war for the military to replace such an odd size. Of course, he couldn't fight without shoes. He was assigned to the Post Office, where he worked happily in sock feet.

The 406th relieved the 30th Infantry Division, and on October 27, the *Journal* records, "The Ozarks had now completed their long march from Texas. They were now on the battlefield for the first time listening to German bullets and shells and applying the techniques of field service learned long ago."[4]

The 102nd Division was to be heavily involved in a campaign deep into Germany and advance on the Rhine at a date to be announced later. It was in this campaign that they first saw combat, especially as they moved to take various towns along the way. On October 31, members of the 406th Infantry captured prisoners and investigated the terrain in North Wurselen, Germany.

In the second week of November, a plan of attack was announced that would include the 102nd in seizing the city of Geilenkirchen. In that campaign, Howard's division would secure Immendorf and prepare to defend it from counterattack by the Germans. On November 12, according to the Infantry Journal, "Company E, 406th Infantry, attacking on the right flank of the battalion's 300-yard front with tanks leading, attempted to envelop Immendorf from the southeast. Company F struck from the left flank, also with close tank support. Moving swiftly, the troops encountered little resistance during the approach to the town. German snipers inside Immendorf fought stubbornly, and it became necessary to carry out a house-by-house mop-up."[5]

Howard was in the middle of the heated battle. At one point, he knew he had to make a dash to a nearby barn for safety, so he ran as fast as he could, bullets kicking up the dirt at his heels. As he turned the corner to get behind the building, the lumber at the corner of the barn was chewed up by German sniper fire, inches from where he had just been. By 2:30 in the afternoon, the mission was over, and the organization of a perimeter defense had begun. "Casualties were light, although four tanks were disabled in passing through a minefield."[6]

On the second day, as a mission to advance further and seize Apweiler, Germany began, an intense hail of enemy artillery, tank guns, mortars, and machine guns halted the attack. The Division was thrown off balance and forced into a defensive position. Meanwhile, a counterattack on the forces holding Immendorf had also begun. "As the attacking Germans slowly advanced on Immendorf, heavy concentrations of artillery and mortar fire quickly broke the enemy formation and destroyed two of the three assaulting companies. Our tank destroyers left three Panther tanks burning." The remaining German soldiers drew closer to the city under the protection of a white flag of truce. However, when they were about a hundred yards out, they dropped the flag and resumed fighting.

Soon, a German tank broke through the defensive line, followed by ground troops, but it was destroyed from 30 yards away by antitank fire. The 3rd Battalion was quickly brought in as reinforcements. The enemy was soon thrown back, and the line was restored around the village.

On the third day, as prisoner interrogation revealed further plans of German counterattack, the order was given to proceed with the plans to capture Apweiler. Through a barrage of artillery fire from a distance, the German infantry occupying the foxholes in Apweiler were trapped and captured without a fight. "The infantry moved steadily through the town, taking a large number of prisoners from the houses as they proceeded; they reached the east side of the town by 1445, and Apweiler was taken."[7]

The success of that mission led the Division deeper into Germany. Around November 21, they were part of the offensive to penetrate into the Rhine. Attacks and counterattacks marked the day, during which Howard's battalion, the 2nd, provided much needed depth to the defense. Despite poor soil and mobility for the equipment, the enemy was defeated, and Maj. Gen. E. N. Harmon "commended the 406th Infantry for having accomplished its missions 'with a dashing and vigorous spirit.'"[8]

Howard's division spent a brutal winter slogging through a ravaged Europe. In February 1945, they arrived at the Ruhr River, a tributary of the Rhine. There, Howard spent fourteen days in a foxhole at 14 degrees below zero. His division was tasked with building a bridge across the river for Allied trucks to cross. Just as they had the bridge built, the Germans blew a dam four miles upriver, washing out the bridge. They had to start over and build another bridge, which they did, and a number of Allied troops crossed successfully into the interior of the Rhineland at that point.

Chapter 4
The Battle of the Bulge

By Christmas 1944, the "Battle of the Bulge" was in full swing. Also known as the "Ardennes Breakthrough," this was a major offensive from the Germans meant to divide the Allied forces west of the Rhine River and to recapture the important harbor of Antwerp. The term "Bulge" refers to the inward bulge of the Allied line on war maps of that battle.

Howard Miskelly still feels that most Americans don't know how close the allies came to being pushed back in that battle, the bloodiest of the war. Due mainly to Nazi aggressiveness, overconfidence of the Allies and poor aerial reconnaissance, the Germans took advantage of bad weather to launch a damaging assault on the Allies' front lines. It was a gamble, though, because it also cost them dearly and depleted their war-making resources.

The Ozarks were well entrenched in the task of holding the defensive line against the advancing German army. The emotions and tensions were heightened on both sides. "The German 59th Infantry Division gradually moved in between the Roer and Wurm rivers. This was a good command, perhaps one of the few remaining topnotch Wehrmacht Divisions. It was led by Major General Poppe, sardonically named "Poppe the Intrepid" by his men and officers because of a previous incident in his military career. At one time he had commanded a division in the Crimea, a division which he was reported to have abandoned in headlong personal flight during the evacuation of that area, leaving his men to their fate.

"General Poppe was now nervous. He had strict orders to divert as many Allied forces as possible from the Ardennes area. Accordingly, he made a show of strength. His patrols were more aggressive under pain of death for missions unaccomplished. Flare after flare illuminated no man's land at night. German sentries were instructed to be more alert-- and to watch each other so that comrades would not desert. Propaganda was shelled over. Broadcasts were beamed at front line Ozarks. On Christmas Eve the Germans played Christmas carols for our benefit, possibly to make the men homesick. The Luftwaffe appeared in increasing numbers, dropping high-explosive and antipersonnel bombs on rear areas. German artillery became more and more frantic, and applied special vengeance on the Puffendorf crossroads where our MPs directed traffic between 150mm shell bursts along the tree-lined road to Linnich. Casualties were light, however, for our troops lived and worked in concrete-and-steel basements which the Germans had long ago built into their schools and houses in the Siegfried Line zone. Every night the deepest basement reverberated as buzz bombs clattered low overhead, bound for Holland and England."[9]

At the beginning of the second week in January, the 102nd Division had made great strides in their offensive initiative, and they clearly held the front. The Allies had been pushed back and could not advance due to the weather. It is rumored that Patton ordered his chaplain to pray for good weather. He did, it came, and as Howard remembers, the sky was filled with bombers, like a cloud, hundreds of them. The Germans had never seen anything like it. The pilots connected with the infantry, and the Allies advanced.

Not far ahead lay an SS camp. Howard and three of his fellow soldiers, called "the Rebels" because they were all from the South, were assigned to spearhead the charge to take the camp. More than 20 elite SS soldiers were holed up in one building, from where they repelled attacks. Howard and the other three made their way up to the building, taking cover and avoiding being shot long enough for two of them to successfully lob hand grenades into the building. The grenades exploded with shattering force, and the building fell silent. Howard and his fellow southerners were told they would receive a Silver Star for their bravery, but the medals never came.

Though some divisions fared better than others, as a whole, the Allies had suffered tremendous casualties in the Battle of the Bulge. A four-star general wanted the 86th Division and Howard's 102nd Division to be ready to go into the heat of the battle. One would go, while the other would remain in reserve. The Division Commander flipped a coin, and the 86th Division went. They suffered a casualty rate of 84%.

While holding their line, the Allied forces were still subjected to the enemy's propaganda. "Leaflets written in Russian, leaflets addressed to the 84th Division, and leaflets directed to British troops were widely shelled over our front lines. By 16 January, Poppe had either recovered his senses or replenished his stock of literature as messages fluttering into Rurdorf were addressed "To the boys of the 102d" and "To the poor devils of the 102d." The Ozarks' only gripe was that there were never enough leaflets to go around. As souvenirs, the demand far exceeded the supply."[10]

As the Allies pushed through to take the Rhineland, the agreement was to stop at the Elbe River and meet the

Russians there. On March 1, the 406th Infantry "moved out from Hardt at 0900 and met scattered resistance until the 2nd Battalion's left flank began to receive 88mm and machine gun fire from the high ground between Viersen and Suchteln."[11] Howard was on the ground with his 24-pound Browning Automatic Rifle. Along with his fellow soldiers, he peered ahead, across the open field and up to the two high points on either side of their objective. Howitzer fire rained down in front of them. This is where their training would pay off. Howard and his partner, a young man from Pennsylvania named Richardson, launched out into the open. Howard fired, ran, hit the ground, rolled, got up, and fired again. He did this continually, zigzagging across the terrain. As he rolled upright, he glanced to his left. Richardson also rolled, knelt, and aimed. Then his chest exploded. He had been shot in the heart. Howard had no choice but to continue on.

As night fell on March 1, the Division successfully possessed Viersen. They had achieved their objective, but Howard keenly felt the loss.

Chapter 5
Battle of Krefeld

By February 24, 1945, the United States Army had made such aggressive progress, that when they reached the Rhine on March 1, they found that the Germans had destroyed all bridges crossing it in an effort to slow them down. This forced the XIX Corps north toward Uerdingen, as they sought to seize the Adolf Hitler bridge intact. "This hope never materialized. When Uerdingen was captured on 3 March by the 95th Infantry Division this bridge, too, had been demolished and lay beneath the swirling waters of the Rhine."[12]

Their subsequent movement northwest took them to the edge of Krefeld on their way to the Rhine eight miles north of Uerdingen. "As a result of this change the Ozarks were pinched out at Krefeld and the maneuver to seize the south half of the city was necessarily limited to only two directions of approach--from the south and southwest.... Hence the situation looked propitious for the capture of this major prize, one of the most important Rhineland cities. On the other hand, on the morning of 2 March when the Division resumed its attack northeast against Krefeld from the general line of the Niers Canal, German forces were still retreating through the city toward Uerdingen. As the Division approached the city enemy opposition became more determined and more skillful in a final desperate effort to retain this escape route."[13]

Howard Miskelly's regiment, the 406th, advanced on the left. The 1st Battalion of the 406th made slow progress along the south side of the Viersen-Krefeld railroad. The Germans were ensconced in heavy patches of woodland and were better able to resist the attack. They skirted around to the west bank of the Niers Canal, where the assistance of the 2nd Battalion helped them cross the Canal and push through Anrath without a fight. When they were just beyond the town, they were greeted by fire from 20mm flak guns on the left flank. Their own tank support, however, "blasted the enemy positions along the railroad and the troops advanced employing assault fire."[14]

As the 1st Battalion approached Krefeld, Company A confronted head-on an entrenched enemy who was ready for them with antitank ditches and machine-gun fire. Company A, though, supported by tanks, took the first line of defense, capturing some sixty prisoners and eighty machine guns. "One German soldier, approaching under a white flag, shot an American soldier; the fight then flared anew and resolved into something approaching 'no quarter asked or given.' At 1530 (3:30 pm) the last enemy capitulated and the advance on the city was resumed."[15]

By the end of the day on March 2, 1945, the enemy was on the run but Krefeld had yet to be fully taken. In order to secure the city, the 2nd Battalion would have to stage a nighttime operation. Howard knew that one of the very worst assignments you can get is a night patrol like this. He tried not to let the growing fear control his movements, but he couldn't help noticing that his mouth was dry and his hands shook a little while he prepared himself for battle. He stretched the black toboggan over his head, hiding all of the white skin that he could so that moonlight would not expose his position. Along with his fellow soldiers, he also put socks on over his shoes to minimize the sound of boots on rocky soil. When they were ready, they set off for the houses of Krefeld. Howard's assignment, with his friends, was to take the city house by house in the black dark of night until they encountered Germans.

Howard had never felt terror like this. The city was completely dark, not a light anywhere. More silently than he ever thought possible, he moved with the others through the darkness, his 24-pound Browning assault rifle shoulder high and trained ahead of him with lethal intensity. As they moved cautiously house to house, clearing them room by room, he never knew if the next opened door would bring the wide eyes of terrified homeowners or the flash of a muzzle, bringing him the last thing that he would ever see. Howard tasted something new, now. It was not quite bitter, it was more metallic, kind of like blood but not exactly. He knew, without having to be told, that he had literally tasted fear.

During the night, almost all of the enemy combatants fled the city. The next morning the advancing combat teams met no resistance, but German communications were badly disrupted. One enemy rifle platoon was captured as they naively approached the city, unaware that their fellow soldiers had already left town. "A German medical officer was also apprehended while calmly walking down the street with his wife. When questioned, he simply remarked, 'I did not know the city had been taken.'" By noon on that day, Krefeld was officially pronounced captured.[16]

According to the Infantry Journal, "From 23 February to 3 March the Ozarks had advanced 33 miles, captured 83 towns and villages, invested 3 cities, and taken 4,187 prisoners. Although enemy resistance had sometimes been light, much stubborn opposition was overcome by resourceful tactics and the vigor and momentum of the attack. The XXIX Tactical Air Command also rendered material assistance by flying 180 sorties and dropping a total of 90 tons of bombs. The battle was not without losses, however, for we suffered 1,888 casualties. Of this number, 178 were killed in action, 1,219 wounded. Non-battle casualties numbered 351."[17]

As the Allies approached the Elbe River to meet the Russians, Howard was surprised to see the Germans rushing toward the Americans on motorcycles, in wagons, and on mules. The Russians had not yet arrived, and the Germans were desperate to be captured by the Americans first.

Chapter 6
Letters From War: Stateside

Camp Wolters, Texas
Nov. 25, 1943

Dear Dad,

I was very glad to get your letter as well as Mother's. I was surprised to hear from you in writing. I guess I rate pretty good to get a few lines from you. I could read it okay.

Well, today is Thanksgiving. I'm not working today, but will Sunday to make up for today. Any day lost in the army must be made up by working Sunday or overtime. Do you remember what we did last Thanksgiving? Well, I do. You plowed across the ditch and I spent the day in walnuts, then Alvis and I went to Ripley and dated some girls. Won't do anything like that today, though, for we are restricted to Camp Wolters area for I don't know how long.

I probably won't get out for Christmas. It will be pretty lonely for me out here, but I will make out some way. I wrote all my girlfriends and told them not to get me a Christmas present for I won't be able to get them one on account of I won't be at any place to get one. That's fair enough, isn't it? They buy me nothing, I get them nothing. I'm not interested in Christmas presents at the present time. There is something more important than presents to me. I'll be glad when this mess is over for I'm paying dear for every day I live. Getting up about five every morning, I'm always drilling at daylight. We fall out in our leggings, helmet liner and work clothes. We have about fifteen minutes to get up, dress in all that stuff, wash our face and hands, make our bed and that ain't last, out here they have inspection every day.

Twice a week we scrub our barracks, carry our beds out to sun, and mop our floors dry, wash the windows, empty all trash out of cans, clean the bath house, and that all must be done after work hours, not on the government's time. I live upstairs and its very un-handy to lug the bed up and down the stairs. Must be done, though.

Now that's the way we go every day. When am I going to have time to write my letters? That doesn't include cleaning our rifles and extra duty. I also catch

62

K.P. when it comes my time. It's hard, though. The rifle we use is the M.L. known as the 30 caliber, put up by the Springfield Company. It's really a find, too. There isn't one in the world better. It will kill far as you can see and further. It don't kick much either.

All my clothes fit pretty good. Arnold and I are at the same place, not in the same company. I have learned to salute all the officers, do a pretty good job of it, too.

Must close now,

Son

Camp Wolters, TX

January 13, 1944

Thursday night

Dear Mom,

How's my dear old Mother and Daddy? With this big snow, bet you all can't hardly keep warm. We are going on range with the BAR (Browning automatic rifle) tomorrow, dread it, too, will get wet and cold. It won't hurt me, though, for I have done it before out here.

Mother, be sure and send Snookie a picture of me, for she is expecting it. Have you all killed both hogs yet? Wish I were there to eat some of that good meat. I got a letter from Roy today, he said that he had volunteered for the army and that he would be leaving any day. Do I believe that? No, I don't. I don't like draft dodgers no matter who it may be. Some day he will be sorry of the fact he didn't do his part. I know enough about fighting to take care of myself alright, and bet I can break his neck in a hand-to-hand fight. We have muscle building exercises every day, and they also teach us dirty fighting, too. Mother, I wouldn't be out of the army to be a draft dodger for anything. It is not fair for some to suffer like I have and others have a good time like the boys around home. I really like the boys here and will miss them when we are separated if we ever are, and I suppose we will be.

It's bedtime now, guess I better go for now, will write soon. I would like a date with a pretty girl. That's impossible, though.

All my love,
Son

Camp Wolters, TX
January 16, 1944
Sunday noon

Dear Mother,

How are you and Daddy getting along, fine, I hope. I am alright as usual. Working pretty hard, though. We finished firing the BAR Saturday noon and didn't work yesterday noon. Had a dance at the USO last night and I went. There was about 200 pretty girls down from Ft. Worth, had a nice time, too.

You mentioned me saving money. I need to save a

little, and am going to. But one thing I won't have to save up for is a furlough, for when I get one, I really won't get a furlough. If I get anything, it will be a delayed travel time from here to P.O.E. (Port of Embarkation) they pay my way back home to the P.O.E. But I don't like to go to a P.O.E. so soon.

I sure would love to see you and Dad long about now, but as with other things, is impossible. Just got back from chow, had a real good dinner. It don't taste good like things you cook, though. I don't know if I will know how to act if I ever do get to come home, for in the army, when they blow the whistle at the table, everybody starts grabbing, so a man has got to be pretty fast to get his part.

Oh yes, I'm on guard duty tonight, the first time ever done guard duty. It's pretty rough, too. Work all night and come in the next morning about daylight, eat chow, and start the day's work, for we have got to work through nights.

You may not get very much mail next week. I better close now, I must dress for guard. We go to guard school before going to guard.

Don't work too hard.

Love,
Son

Camp Wolters
April, 1944
Friday noon

Dear Mother and Dad,

How are both of you today? I am still not working very hard though I filled up some foxholes yesterday and dug some today. I bet Dad has already started farming, or is it still raining there? It's pretty hot here, and they say it gets as high as 120 degrees in the shade. I sure hope they see fit to move me before then, of course one never knows when he may be shipped. May be tonight, and again it may be two months. Third is shipping the 20th of this month. They sure are glad, too. The Cpl. that I took my training under is shipping. He is a good friend of mine. When I go anywhere he usually goes along.

Mother, do you have an extra gas coupon? A man from Mississippi drove his car here and don't have any gas so if we had the gas we could go to town in his car. His wife is here but he would carry me to town, and that certainly would beat waiting an hour for a camp bus. They are so crowded I can hardly get to town. In fact, around an army camp, transportation is pretty tough.

Mother, did I tell you that I bought a new suit of clothes? Well, I did. It is really a pretty suit, too. It is a gabardine material dress suit. Don't ask what it cost. What is money to a man in the army if he can't buy what he wants? And I did want this pretty suit. Although it did

66

cost quite a bit, I bought it after payday, so I didn't miss the money, but I am broke now. That's a soldier's life, to be broke. That little thing doesn't worry me very much.

Does Elva get to come home often? I hope so anyway. I would really like to see everyone along about now. Maybe it won't be too long before I get home. By the way, a soldier gets 10 days now instead of 7. That's alright, too. I had better close now and return to work. Hope you and Dad have a nice Easter Sunday and I will be thinking of you both. Do you have a new outfit for Sunday?

Must close now. Love both of you,

Son

Camp Livingston, LA

July 16, 1944

Sunday A.M.

Dear Mother and all,

How's things going around home? I'm on guard at the present time, and I was last night (Sat). I will get off at ten today. Has it rained very much up there yet? Come another shower here the other day so it isn't so hot now.

We are going out Tuesday. I believe it is for three or four days. Pretty soon, we will be leaving on maneuvers then. You won't hear from me for some time, but just remember that I'm doing okay and don't worry about me. I got a birthday card from Elva, too. I appreciate you all thinking of my birthday as it means so little to me because I will work the just the same as any other day except I will be on K.P. tomorrow and I'm not every day. I remember what I did last year on my birthday night. Arnold and I dated Mary Pitney and Ann Street for the first time. You ask if I was angry with Ann for not coming after me. Well, I surely am in fact so angry that I haven't written her since I came back, and it was Martha that brought the radio for me. I surely do use it, too. I'm going to send it home next week as I can't carry it with me. You asked about a box, I think I can get a box. It would be worth a try anyway, don't you think?

I'm very unlucky, both times I had guard it was on Saturday night. Wasn't very much to do, though. I may as well be doing that as well as nothing, I guess. I may as well close, as I know nothing else to write. Bet you haven't got up yet, it's about seven o'clock.

Love,

Son

Chapter 7
Letters From War: The European Theater

October 8, 1944

Dear Folks,

Here is that letter I've been meaning to write but haven't had time until now. I got one letter from home at my other station, sure did enjoy it, too. This place is okay. Good food, in fact the best I've had since I got in the army. The climate is good except I have a cold, which is very uncommon for me. At the present, I am on the east coast. Where, you will get to guess. Don't worry about me, for I'll be okay. I can't say very much in this letter but I can always tell you I'm doing fine, and that's about all that matters. How is Daddy's arm doing? Hope it gets better soon.

You can write this address and I will get it. Use one

V-mail and one regular, I believe that will work okay.

Is Elva coming home very often, sure hope so. Wish I could be there for awhile, but I've got my orders. May as well make the best of it.

Love,
Son

October 10, 1944

Dear Folks,

Well, I guess you was about to decide that I had forgotten you all. No! Just been a bit busy in the past weeks, and besides, as long as you don't hear from me, I'm doing fine so don't worry. Things are about the same with me as ever, nothing new. Food better than before and a good place to sleep, that's worth lots, too. How is everything back home by now? I was near a radio and was able to listen to the World Series. Enjoyed it, too. Did you and Dad hear them? Really sounds good to hear someone talk that is in the States. Don't let anyone tell you the U.S. isn't a swell place. I know, I've been both places. Although England isn't bad at all, it's just something about the States that I like.

I still haven't got any mail yet. Sort of lonesome here without it, too. Lots of the fellows have received mail but I haven't. Guess I will soon, though. I haven't written to Elva since I been over here. Guess I better do that, too, or she will be very angry with me. Mother, don't expect me to send a Christmas present because I won't be able to send one, although I will be thinking of you and Daddy with all of my heart, and will make up for this when I get back. That is going to be some wonderful day when everyone begins to return.

Hope you heard form Curtis since I left. I haven't. I guess he wrote but it hasn't caught up with me yet. He should be through by now, hope he makes it alright.

I think the boys are doing pretty well over here, don't you? Do you ever see Martha these days? Don't suppose Ann Street ever comes around does she? How many cows do you have now? How are my cows doing? How about Sarge? Do you still carry cotton on his back? How many bales are you making this year? What's the price of cotton? These questions may sound silly to you, but I don't know them unless someone tells me, for they don't have cotton quotations where I'm at now.

Just had a bath, feel lots better now. Mother, do you remember those two big warts on my finger? I had them cut off, if you remember. Now there are nine on my finger. I guess they multiply, so I better not have this cut off.

The last report I had on Brownie, she was really shiny. I bet there is lots of girls who know that car, well someday they are going to be surprised when they look and see I'm in there instead of Dad, and I hope that day won't be too long off.

Better close now. All my love,
Son

October 13, 1944

Dear Mother and Daddy,

How's everything back home? Today is Friday the 13th. Wonder if it will be unlucky for me? It really rained here yesterday and everything is wet and muddy, but today is sunny and reminds me of home. I got six letters yesterday, five from Martha and one from you. Oh yes, and one from Arnold but it was sent to Camp Livingston so it is pretty old. I am going to write him from here and it will go direct to him. Martha said it had been some pretty good weather so far and hope it continues that way.

You see by my paper that writing material isn't too plentiful. I remember when I used this type of paper back in the 6th grade. Seems like a long time. Martha wrote me a mail and said that she had got the paper for Neil last Christmas and didn't send it, but never expected to be using it the way she is now, so you see a lot can happen in a year.

There is a lot more to do over here than one would expect. They have dances and the Red Cross gives little shows, so we go there sometimes. I better close and write someone else to let them know I'm doing fine. Keep writing and let me know all the latest news.

All my love,
Son

April 11, 1945

Dear Mother,

Today has been a very easy day for me. When I got up this morning it was pouring rain. In fact, it has been raining for the past three days. Mother, from what I can hear on the radio, the Pacific War is coming along fine. I'm a pessimistic man, I look for the worst and when good happens, I've got a good surprise.

I guess you have heard about the education for soldiers overseas. Well, it's a bunch of crap, just something to announce over the radio so the people back home can hear it. Sure, we have a class twice a week, but have no books, no nothing. Although I do have a good subject-- soil condition and crop management. I also have a good instructor. My instructor was a county agent for 4 years and he also attended college for three years. He really knows his stuff. I wouldn't mind having a farm and some other work, too. I was taking radio but am having it changed to livestock production. The work I do now may be entered on college record, that is if I go.

Roy has more trouble than anyone I know. No, I don't think he lost it, what I think is he spent it just like I always did. He and Elmer changes their mind more than anyone I know. I can't understand why some people are so lucky, for Roy has had his part of luck, too. He has had a good chance to make good while most everyone was in the service.

So long, from

Son

June 21, 1945

Dear Mother and Dad,

How's things going with you all? It's a rainy day here. We started to play a double header ball game but didn't get the last one finished because of rain. We aren't doing very much work, just keeping busy mostly.

Looks like we may stay over here as occupation, I hope we do, too, that's much easier than some things there is to do. Yesterday the Red Cross girls came around with some donuts. I got some paper from them as I didn't have any. Will you please send me some writing paper, envelopes, and about three cans of good brown shoe polish. Also put a shoe brush in. You know we are back in garrison now so everything must be shiny and neat. We may move from here to "Frankfurt." Hope we do because I would like to see that town. It is a very large one, they say. So far I have seen a portion of northern Germany and several parts of southern Germany. It is much nicer here in the south, beautiful hills and everything green. Mother, I have been sending Martha and other things. She will give you a copy after having them reprinted.

How's Dad doing? Bet he is working like mad, you too. One thing I want to tell you and Dad: I'm over here fighting because I want to get back home and live with people I love and enjoy being with, so don't kill yourself working. Money isn't everything. So many people don't realize this until it's too late. If it wasn't for my people at home, I wouldn't care what happened, so take care of yourself for me if for no other reason.

No news, so I'll close for the evening. Tell everyone hello for me.

Love,
Son

June 24, 1945

Dear Mother,

Today has been a usual day for me, last night wasn't so good, though. I pulled guard in a town about four miles away. I got one letter this evening, was from "Grammie." I enjoy her letters, too. Poor thing, she thinks I can't read them, but I can, very easy.

This is a pretty good picture of me, was taken in a small village. You should be getting some from Martha now, I sent her several.

Mother, I just can't tell yet what I am going to do. First I'm in the 9th Army, then they put 102 in the 7th

Army and the latest is we are in the 3ʳᵈ Army, so it keeps a fellow really guessing. But I believe I have a good chance of staying here at least two more months. It sounds funny to hear a fellow say he doesn't want to come home, but it is altogether different when there is another war to fight. I'm not afraid, but not at all anxious to fight the Japanese. Looks good down here now. They say we are ahead of schedule. They hope we continue to advance.

We had a good USO show last week. I really enjoyed it.

They say we may move to Frankfurt, where Ike's regiment is, I don't know. Doesn't really matter. We do training here just as we did in the States, just as hard, too. Is Burbin Cross out of the army for good, or just got a leave? Looks as if Elmer may get a chance to fight the Japanese. You know four months isn't long to take training, guess he would be like Roy and get out some way. Arnold finally broke down and wrote a long letter, telling of all the fun he had while taking those prisoners. I had quite a time myself.

So long for now. Don't work too hard.

Love,
Son

July 9, 1945

Dear Mother,

I'm sorry I haven't written before now, but don't be angry, I have a good reason for not. We have moved about three times, and for six days we lived in pup tents, which didn't give me a chance to write. It rained every day we were there, boy, what a mess. And for this place where we are now, it isn't any better. I don't know the name because it's too small. It really stinks, not a good house in the whole village and the bad part is it looks now like we will be here for at least one month and maybe longer. I think I'm in the 3rd Army now, and if so I may be occupation, this is only my belief, not official. I'm in the extreme southern part of the country, just a few lines form the Czech border. I might even get to go over there, kindly hope I do. We have a new company commander now. Boy, we sure did lose a good man, too. I don't know how this one will be.

I haven't had any mail for 10 days so I don't know the latest at home. Hope all are as good as myself, except for being lonesome for the sight of my people. Never did get the package you sent, probably will soon. Will you please send another? I thought for a while I wouldn't send for any more because I would probably come home soon but as things are working now it may be awhile yet. Kindly hope it is. I can sweat days out here much easier than in combat. Don't let anyone kid you, "War is rough," every single day of it.

We played a ball game today. Won, too. Did I tell you that our company has the best team in the battalion?

Yes, we won the tournament. How's my Dad? Tell him I can read his letters too, so write. Really, I enjoy reading them. Things are so inconvenient here, it's hard to write a letter, but I'll try later.

Your Son,
Howard

August 12, 1945

Dear Mother and all,

No news of excitement has happened here since I last wrote you. Mother, if your mail is half as slow as my mail, you don't get much. I received the letters in two weeks. I know you write lots, and so does Martha, but I get none. Say, the news sounds terribly good just now, and by the time you get this, they will probably be back where they started from. Frankly, I don't think the Japs will accept the offer.

Mother, there is two of the cutest little boys live up the street from here. They know my name and when they see me they come running. They are always so clean and their hair combed so cute. There is also lots of cute girls over here. Mother, you have probably heard over the radio about "fraternization." Well, you need not worry about me nor no one else because the boys aren't in love with the girls. This is one thing I don't like about newspapers, they try to get people back home angry about something like this. It's silly when they write big columns in the paper telling how the boys act over here. As a whole, it's darn good conduct. Put a group of Americans together and you have a pretty good bunch of men. Sure, we are going to talk to them a little, it's natural, but no more now than when it was forbidden.

One of the boys got a package today so we eat good. Mother, you spoke of the package situation some time ago. It's good as a whole, I finally got all the packages you sent. Boy, some of them were really smashed up.

Guess Dad isn't working so hard now, at least if I were there I wouldn't be. Tell him to take a break and not work too hard.

So long, Mom.

Love,
Son

(Author's note: the following letter was written on V-J Day, the day that World War II officially ended.)

August 15, 1945

Dear Mother,

This is a day that will be long remembered. Yes, it's what we have been waiting on for a long time. I'm very glad it's here. Maybe in the near future a good part of the boys can get home and out of the army. Me being over here, I don't know just when I will get home, probably in early '46. It's quite a while yet but I can wait now that our boys aren't being murdered by the thousands.

It's been hard to stay away from you and Dad for so long. I have been in some terrible places, but God has always got me through. It seems impossible for the whole world to be at peace and no war. I tell you, it's a grand feeling.

Of course I can't celebrate now, and haven't got anything to look forward to in the next few months. But I guess we couldn't all be home. This may help Neil a lot, at least it should. It will be nice when he and Elva can be happy again. I haven't been able to see Curtis yet, don't know when I can, either, he hasn't answered my last letter yet. Transportation is bad over here.

I'll close now, Mom. I'm always thinking of home and hope it isn't too long now.

Love,
Son

August 22, 1945

Dear Mother,

I received a letter from you today. At that time, the war was almost over. And now, well it is a grand thing to say, although it's very hard to realize, me being over here and not being able to do anything extra. And now for the history of myself in the past couple of days.

I have been doing about the same as usual. It rains lots and we don't work when it is wet. To be truthful, we don't hurt ourself at any time, just enough to say we are busy. There is no change in the training schedule as before the end of the war. In fact, one unit is going on maneuvers pretty soon. This will continue until I become a civilian again. How long this will be, I don't know. There is talk of us moving, but no one knows where as yet.

In this letter today, Elva was home and you all were having a good time. I also received a letter from Martha today and was she happy about getting to come to my house (as she called it), says everything was perfect. Well, almost everything, anyway!! She is crazy about all of you and Daddy especially. While I'm away, said he looks more like me every day. Of course, this is flattering me.

As you can tell, there isn't anything to write about but I try and tell everything I know. Martha doesn't think I tell her enough, said I haven't even told her of our new bathroom. She liked it a lot, too. I can't wait to get back, everything is perfect now. This may mean I won't ever leave home.

Love,
Son

Chapter 8
The Occupation Years

When World War II was finally declared over on August 15, 1945, Howard was in no particular hurry to get home. Sure, he had exchanged letters regularly with Martha Rae and Ann, but he had no commitment to either of them, really. There was no wife and family waiting for him, and no one was shooting at him anymore, so why not live in Europe for a while and be paid by Uncle Sam to do it? So, Howard Miskelly signed up to join the Occupation force of the United States Army.

Howard was sent immediately to Selb. Selb was in the state of Bavaria, in the east central region of Germany, very near the border of Czechoslovakia. He was assigned as the staff sergeant managing the Officer's Quarters there, supervising six other officers. Together they lived in a 7-story hotel that was now vacant due to the war. It was just the seven of them, and they had the entire hotel to themselves. Howard arranged for their food and other daily needs to be met, so that made him the mother hen.

While living in Selb, Howard also learned that they had been famous for their manufacture of some of the finest china in the world. The factories had all been shut down by the war now, but Howard had an idea. He approached the owners of these china factories and asked if they would make more.

"Sure," they said, " but we have no coal. You get us the coal, we will make you some china."

Howard was now on a mission bigger than the army's. He looked around everywhere he could for coal, and he finally found a trainload of it, just sitting there, waiting to be taken away. It was, of all places, in a town called Falkner, Czechoslovakia.

Howard acquired the whole train for free, and had it taken to Selb.

"That's fine coal," they said, "and we can use it. We'll get started right away."

It took over a week for the kilns of Selb to get fired up, but when they were, Howard commissioned his prize. In all, they made, specifically for Howard Miskelly, seven sets of beautiful, one-of-a-kind very fine china, 144 pieces in all.

Compared to the fear and the heat of battle, occupation was the easy life. The civilians were all glad the soldiers were there, and since the soldiers also carried a gun, the people were happy to defer to them in all matters. Before long, Howard and another officer devised a plan that would help them make the best of being there. A young officer from Montgomery, Alabama, First Lieutenant Auberly, had a proposition.

"Hey, Howard," Auberly said, "I got an idea."

"What's that?" said Howard.

"You remember telling me how you and your friend at home ran his daddy's mail route every now and again?"

"I do," he said.

"Well," said Auberly, "what if we ran a different kind of route?"

"How do you mean?"

"I mean, all us soldiers get sent all this chocolate and cigarettes every month, and lots of the boys don't even smoke. I hear there's quite a market for those things out in the civilian population. What do you say we do some business? I can get us a jeep. Why don't you get us a trailer and let's make some investments?"

Howard agreed that it was a good idea. Auberly got the jeep, Howard got the trailer, and together they established a route where they would buy the unwanted cigarettes from the soldiers, who were happy to sell them. Howard and Auberly paid them $20 per carton, and they were ecstatic. If they didn't smoke, what use were they anyway? In turn, Howard and Auberly would sell them to a man in town who paid them $100 per carton. It was all Occupation money anyway, and it was floating around everywhere. Some of it was German, some Russian, and some of it probably counterfeit, but it was there, and they made it work for them.

In short order, Howard literally had more money than he knew what to do with. In accordance with army policy, he was given one APO number, with which he could send money home. The problem, though, was that the amount of money he could send back to the States was limited to what he was being paid by the army, namely about $154 per month. Auberly had the same problem. As they were talking about it, Auberly smiled.

"I think I know a guy," he said.

Auberly did indeed know a guy in military administration, and one day he came into the hotel and handed Howard a piece of paper. "There you are, my friend. Problem solved."

"What's this?" Howard said, scanning the sheet of paper.

"That there's your saftey net, Howie. Seven more APO numbers. Send home as much money as you want."

Eventually, Howard was assigned to duty in Ash, Czechoslovakia, in the no man's land known as

Sudetenland. Sudetenland, which gets its name from the Sedenes Mountains around it, is a stretch of land about eighteen miles long that belongs to whomever is in power at the moment in eastern Europe. When Germany was in power, it was theirs, but now, after the war, it had reverted back to its rightful owner, Czechoslovakia.

Howard enjoyed his life in Ash, including riding with his buddy on a big motorcycle, to the Czech capital of Prague. It was a beautiful country, with no more war, and Howard let the wind blow through his hair and his soul at the same time.

On the day that Howard returned home from the war, he walked up to the farm that he had not seen in years. At the other end of a one-acre plot, his father was plowing. Homer Miskelly saw his son, threw the lines off over his head, and came running, full out. He hit Howard at almost full speed, throwing his arms around his son and weeping. Howard's mother saw him running, and was not far behind. And there, in the rich and precious dirt of north Mississippi, Howard and his mother and father held each other, and cried, and cried, and cried.

Howard in uniform, 1943

Digging in on the approach to Krefeld

Howard is in this group of men resting after reaching Ersleben.

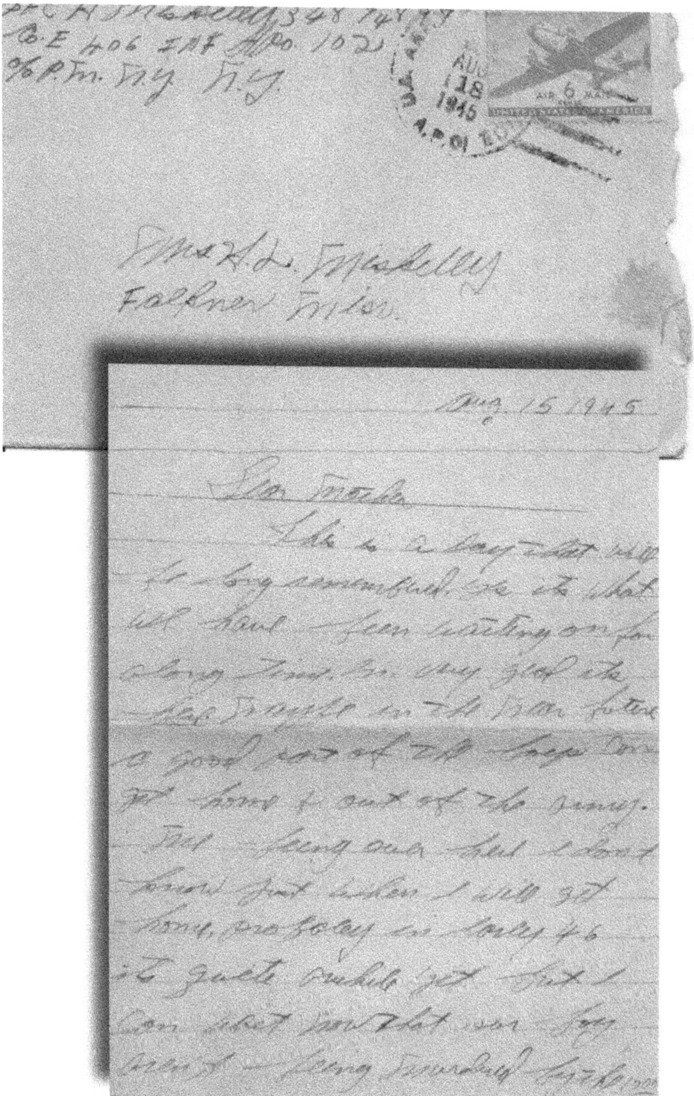
Aug. 15 1945

Dear Mother

This is a day that will be long remembered. It is what we have been waiting on for a long time. I'm very glad it's [illegible] in the near future a good part of the boys can get home & out of the army.

[illegible] being over here I don't know just when I will get home, probably in early 46 [illegible]

Howard's letter home on V-J Day, 1945.

Howard Miskelly   MOST POPULAR BOY

Union University's
Most Popular Boy

The happy and eager staff of *Howard's* circa 1951.

A painting from a friend, depicting Howard's three favorite places: *Howard's* in Okolona, the First Baptist Church, and his home.

Howard and Ann at the opening of the Howard L. Miskelly Recruitng Center in the South End Zone at Mississippi State University.

FITTING HONOR

Miskelly, 88, awarded Bronze Star for World War II service

Howard Miskelly, 88, acknowledges family, friends and officials after being awarded the Bronze Star on Friday at the state Capitol in Jackson. Miskelly, a retired staff sergeant and furniture business owner, was presented with the medal and an American flag that flew over the U.S. Capitol for his service with the 102nd Infantry Division during World War II. GREG JENSON/THE CLARION-LEDGER

By Therese Apel
tapel@jackson.gannett.com

Howard Miskelly has long been a familiar name in Mississippi, as his furniture business is well-known, but on Friday at the state Capitol the retired Army staff sergeant was recognized for service to his country.

In front of a large gathering of family, friends and the media, the 88-year-old veteran was given the Bronze Star for his service in World War II, when the 102nd Infantry Division fought in Belgium, Holland and Germany. His division saw 932 members killed, 2,668 wounded and 150 who died from their wounds.

Gov. Phil Bryant pointed out that his own father, D.C. Bryant, joined the Navy about the same time Mis-

kelly joined the Army.

"The Greatest Generation like Howard Miskelly and the D.C. Bryants of the world saw the tragedy

> *"People ask me if I was frightened over there, but when you're 20 years old you're not scared of anything. When I got back home and saw what had happened, I said, 'My goodness, that was terrible.'"*
>
> **HOWARD MISKELLY,** 88, who was awarded the Bronze Star on Friday

See STAR, Page 2A

92

The Howard and Meme Miskelly clan.

Some family members who may not have made it into the group photo!

The life-size bronze statue of Howard Miskelly, sculpted by Ron Wanek. The statue now resides in the flagship Miskelly Furniture store in Pearl, Mississippi.

CHAPTER 9
Joe College

When Howard Miskelly walked into the Bank of Falkner upon leaving the army, he was recognized as one of their biggest depositors. In his account was some $15,000 that he had sent home. "Mr. Conner!" yelled the receptionist. "Howard Miskelly is here!"

Since he had been drafted right after high school, Howard now promptly enrolled in Union University, a Christian school in Jackson, Tennessee, about an hour north of Falkner. A train called *The Rebel* ran from Mobile, Alabama to Jackson, Tennessee, and back. Howard could catch it on Friday evening in Jackson and ride it to Falkner, then get back on early Monday morning and ride back to Union. He came home on the weekends and went to church with his family, but the anchor for his spiritual life was now being found at school.

Howard's solid Christian heritage had influenced his decision, and after arriving at Union, he did not regret it. As part of the regular school schedule, the students were required to attend chapel services every day, and Howard loved it. He saw how happy the other students were in their sincere and complete devotion to the Lord, and it challenged him. Although Howard had believed in Jesus since childhood, and in fact had never doubted all the way through the army, he realized at Union that he had never made a conscious decision to surrender his life to Jesus and live for him alone. Seeing his fellow students at Union cemented that for him. He was soon baptized in a cow pond, and he never looked back.

One of Howard's friends at Union University was a young man named Duane Pope. Duane's father was a doctor not far from Jackson, Tennessee. Howard and Duane had been told that a freshman was to arrive from Arkansas, but that he had gotten as far as Jackson and had fallen ill. Howard and Duane went to visit him in the hospital. He was a very likeable young man, and he told them that his parents would be there to sit with him the next day.

In a few days, Howard and Duane went to visit him again. It was on this visit that it was impressed upon Howard that a good education is essential. "Hello again," said Duane, "did your parents ever make it here to see you?"

"Well," said the young man, "if they have came, I have not saw them." Howard smiled. The boy from Arkansas had already told them that he was planning on majoring in English.

Howard Miskelly and Arnold Wayne Rowland were double first cousins. Howard can't remember now how that came to be, but there it was. They grew up together, fast friends, and Howard liked hanging around with him, because, as Howard says, Arnold Wayne was movie star handsome, and all the girls agreed. It occurred to Howard that being friends and cousins with Arnold Wayne was not a bad thing, seeing as how he got to hob nob with all of the prettiest girls in town who couldn't get close enough to his cousin.

Howard and Arnold Wayne were close for many years, and they both went to Union University in Jackson, Tennessee on basketball scholarships. Arnold Wayne was even taller than Howard, which added to the movie star mystique. After just a few weeks at Union University, Arnold Wayne was ready to leave.

"I can't stay here, Howard. This isn't working out," he said.

"What do you mean?" replied Howard. "This is a great place!"

"Yes, it is that," said Arnold Wayne. "It's just that I'm

not really cut out for the whole school thing. It's not for me. I can't stay."

"Well what are you going to do?" asked Howard.

"Well," said Arnold Wayne, "I thought I might go to Memphis and get a job with Delta Airlines, as a baggage handler or something.:

"Okay, if that's what you want, I guess. I sure will miss you around here."

And with that, Arnold Wayne Rowland went off in a new direction. He did, in fact, get a job as a baggage handler with Delta, and in the years to come, he worked his way up in the organization until he became the head of Food Services for Delta Airlines.

In the first days of 1967, Arnold Wayne was at a revolving restaurant in Montgomery, Alabama, when someone used the wrong cleaning compounds. In a spark and a flash, the restaurant exploded, killing Arnold Wayne among others. Howard grieved his lifelong friend, and wrote the following letter to Arnold Wayne's widow and children:

February 20th, 1967
Dear Hope, Lynn and Scott:

Hope, you and your children have been in my prayers since Arnold's death. I did not realize that I loved Arnold like I did. Arnold and I, as you know, were raised like brothers, went to the Army together and then to College together. I keep remembering all the things we did together during those times and all the funny things that he has said. To know Arnold was to love him and because of his sense of humor, people loved to be around him.

We have but one regret, that is the fact that we were not able to come and visit you as we had wanted to do.

Knowing Arnold to be a good Christian, I can resign myself to knowing he is far happier now being with our Lord. It is hard for us left, but God is ever ready to take us in His arms and comfort and strengthen us. Have faith in Him, knowing that someday we will see Arnold again.

If you should ever need me, do not hesitate to call on me as I will be ready to help you any way that I can.

We wish you all would plan to come see us in our new home. We are very proud of it and are enjoying living in it so much.

God bless you all now, and I am sure with His help you can find the comfort and strength you need at this time.

Love to all,
Howard

Howard Miskelly spent two wonderful years at Union, and they gave him a direction and a grounding in spiritual integrity that would stay with him forever. That being said, he wasn't always the most accomplished student. That fact, though, ended up working very much to his favor.

One summer, after making a "D" in Chemistry, he found himself going to Blue Mountain Girls School, about 15 miles from Falkner, to make up the course. Now that he was back home, he had been seeing Ann Street again, and she was going to Blue Mountain, too. By this time, after the war, his friendship with Martha Rae had become just that, a friendship that made her more like a sister, while his relationship with Ann had blossomed into real life romance. As they rode back and forth to Blue Mountain every day that summer, their conversations deepened, and so did their love. It was on one of those rides home that Howard Miskelly asked Ann Street if she would be his wife.

Howard and Ann were married in the Spring of 1948 in a small, pretty wedding at Ann's home in Ripley, Mississippi. It was a perfect spring day, and the scent of magnolias and honeysuckle wafted across the small assembly as their vows were made before God, family, and friends.

Howard had booked their honeymoon at the famous Peabody Hotel in Memphis, well known at that time as the finest hotel in the South. After the wedding and reception, Howard and Ann headed for the hotel, arriving just after 7:00 pm. As they entered the lobby to register, Ann soon realized that they would not be going to their room right away. Joe Louis, "The Detroit Bomber," was boxing, and Howard hovered over the radio to listen to the fight.

Howard and Ann did have a wonderful honeymoon in Memphis, but it wasn't a complete getaway. Howard had to spend some of the time studying for a chemistry final exam that he would be taking as soon as they returned.

After Howard finished his two years at Union, he and Ann moved to Starkville, Mississippi, where he had transferred to Mississippi State University to study Agriculture. It was difficult to find a place to live, but some friends of Ann's mother stepped in and helped. They moved into a nice little apartment, where they would stay for two years.

It was during Howard's pursuit of a degree in Agriculture that he met and became friends with a man named Jerry Clower. Jerry would go on to become a world famous comedian and a member of the Grand Ole Opry, and record 28 full-length comedy albums with MCA Records. Two of those records would be certified gold, meaning they each sold more than a million copies. Hints of Jerry Clower's future exploits were evident, though, when he was in school at Mississippi State.

In one particular instance, Jerry drew on the cultural

popularity of the nearby women's college, Mississippi State College for Women, or MSCW, which was located in Columbus, about 20 miles from Starkville, and whose campus saw frequent visits from the young men at Mississippi State. Howard and Jerry shared a Sociology class taught by a man named Professor Cain. After a particularly important exam, Dr. Cain addressed Jerry when the papers were given back.

"Mr. Clower," said Dr. Cain, "may I read to the class your answer to the last question on the exam?"

"Yessir," said Jerry, "you certainly may."

Dr. Cain adjusted his glasses and cleared his throat before he read aloud. "'What,'" he began, "makes a wildcat wild?' And Mr. Clower's answer? 'The same thing that makes the boys go to MSCW!'"

During his time at Mississippi State, Howard put his army experience to good use. He became the ROTC Cadet Colonel, which afforded him an invitation to a grand banquet, and the opportunity to walk under upheld swords with Miss MSU on his arm. He served as the president of his fraternity, and was eventually given a direct appointment by the President of the United States to a post in the regular army at Fort Bragg. Howard had a chance to be career military, but other loves called.

It was also at Mississippi State, though, that the leadership skills Howard learned in the army began to benefit him here at home. Howard was completing a minor in landscape gardening when he had a class with about eighty other students. Two weeks before the final exam, the professor had told the class that for the many plants that they would have to identify, they could use the common name for that plant, and that he was not going to require them to know the scientific names of each. Howard was relieved to hear it.

On the day of the final exam, the tests were given out, and the first thing Howard noticed was that the exam was exactly the opposite of what they had been told. They were not to use common plant names, but were now required to use the scientific ones. The problem was that none of them had studied those. Howard stood and took his test up to the teacher.

"Excuse me, Professor?" he said.

"Yes, Mr. Miskelly? How can I help you?"

"Well, sir," said Howard, "you told us two weeks ago that the scientific names would not be on this final exam, but here they are. We studied, but not that."

The professor shrugged. "I changed my mind," he said.

"Well," said Howard, "if I may, sir, that isn't fair at all. You can't just change your mind like that."

"I beg to differ," said the teacher, "I most certainly can, and you are going to take this test."

Eighty pairs of eyes and ears were intently trained on the front of the room. Howard stood up straighter and spoke again. "No, sir, I am not going to take this test." Howard turned to the class. "What I am going to do, is go to the Dean's office and see what he has to say about this. If anyone wants to go with me, you are welcome to do so." With that, he held the exam and left the room. The other eighty followed.

They walked across campus en masse, went directly to the Dean's office, and knocked on his door. "Dr. Snowden," said Howard, " we would like to talk to you for a moment, sir."

Dr. Snowden met with the students as Howard aired their grievance. He nodded, and addressed the group of students. "Is there anyone here," he said, "who would not be content to get a 'C' in this course?"

They all agreed that they would be satisfied with that grade.

"Alright," he said, "it's done. You may go."

A week later, Howard received a letter from Dr. Snowden, summoning him to his office. Howard knew he was in trouble. He was scared, but it was a different kind of scared than he had experienced in Germany. His life was not in the balance here, but his future might be.

Howard arrived at the appointed time, knocked on the door, and walked into Dean Snowden's office. The Dean didn't say a word, he just handed Howard a sheet of paper. Howard was confused, but he began reading. It was a letter that read:

Dear Dr. Snowden,

Please send me your best Agriculture student to apply for the position of teacher here at my school.

Sincerely,

P.W. Gibson, Principal

Pontotoc High School

Dr. Snowden spoke to Howard when it was clear that he had finished reading. "Mr. Miskelly," he said, "who do you think he's talking about?"

Howard grinned. "He's talking about me, sir."

Dean Snowden returned the smile. "Indeed he is. Now, take that piece of paper and go see him. And good luck to you, Mr. Miskelly."

With that letter, upon his graduation, Howard took what he considered to the very best Agriculture job in the state of Mississippi--a teacher at Pontotoc High School. The pay was very good, and it was only about an hour from Ripley. Howard had learned in the army that leaders take risks. He had done so here, and it had certainly paid off.

Before he graduated, Howard and Ann started another phase of life as their baby girl, Pam, came into the world. Now a family of three, the Miskellys packed up their belongings and moved west to the town of Pontotoc, where Howard would begin a stint as the Agriculture teacher at Pontotoc High.

Howard was told by others on staff there that his predecessor just could not get along with Mr. Gibson, the superintendent. Again, his army training was engaged. Howard had known plenty of officers who were hard to please, but he had learned the secret of getting along with difficult people: if at all possible, just do what they want you to do.

Howard went to Pontotoc and he did everything that Mr. Gibson wanted him to do, and more. Before long, Howard was telling Mr. Gibson what to do, and Gibson was never the wiser. Howard had long ago learned the principles of servant leadership, and once again, it was helping him get ahead. It even led to Howard's making more money than what the school system paid. Mr. Gibson owned a hotel in McComb, and he hired Howard to landscape it for him.

On top of that, Howard's status as a veteran also earned him extra income. At the school, he only taught three 45-minute classes a day. That left him with enough time to lend his expertise to overseeing various Veteran's classes, paying another $100 per month each.

Life was good for the little Miskelly family, but soon, Howard and Ann were about to stumble into their life's calling, and it had nothing to do with dairy farming, movie theaters, the military, education, or agriculture. They were about to enter the world of retail sales.

CHAPTER 10
Dress for Success

Howard Miskelly now had a wife and a baby, and he was making a good living as a high school Agriculture teacher and overseeing classes for veterans. On Saturdays he had another role, though, as he straightened his tie and prepared to meet customers. Because on Saturdays, Howard was a salesman at *Christ Brothers* department store in downtown Pontotoc.

Howard had never been in sales before, but he found that he not only liked it, but he had a knack for it. He had always been personable and a good listener, and people seemed to innately like him and trust him. And he was, in fact, trustworthy. Howard preferred personal interactions with people over making a dollar, so he treated them with respect and never pressured someone to buy something that they didn't want.

Christ Brothers was next door to a clothing store named Gordon's, owned by a Mr. Gordon, or rather Gordinsky, a Russian Jew who had come to America some years before with two of his brothers, looking for a life in the land of opportunity. He changed his name to Gordon to make it more palatable to the American tongue. Gordon was close to 90 years old, and neither he nor his wife could drive a car.

Howard worked at Christ Brothers through 1950 and '51, and he discovered a love for retail clothing sales. In late 1951, the kindly Mr. Gordon announced that he was ready to finally retire, so he had a conversation with his favorite next-door neighbor's employee.

"Howard," he said, "you know how much I like and respect you, don't you?"

"Well, I hope you know that I feel the same about you, sir."

"And," continued Gordon, "I don't know if you've noticed, but I'm not getting younger. 90 years is long enough to work, don't you think?"

"Oh, Mr. Gordon, you're still a spring chicken. You'll be around..."

"No, Howard," Gordon laughed. "You don't lie to the customers, so don't start with me. I am retiring, Howard, and I would like to know if you would like to buy the store in Okolona from me."

Howard was flattered, surprised, excited, and more

than a little scared. But he had been scared before. He enjoyed his teaching job, but he knew he had found his calling here. "I--I don't know what to say..."

"Say 'yes.'"

"I think I want to. May I talk it over with Ann first?"

"I would yell at you if you didn't," said the old man. "Let me know as soon as you can, though. I'm ready to start my retirement years."

Having lived with Howard for a few years now, Ann was as sure as Howard that retail was where he belonged, and here he was, offered his own store in a place where people already knew and trusted him, and where there was a ready-made customer base. Still, Howard and Ann not only talked it over, they prayed about it. And they didn't make a decision until they had peace in their hearts and minds about what God wanted them to do. Although they felt good about this direction, they didn't have any money with which to buy a clothing store.

So, Howard approached Ann's great uncle, who was an eye doctor and who also owned a jewelry store. Mr. Gordon's selling price was $10,000.00. Ann's great uncle gladly agreed to the loan, and Howard accepted Mr. Gordon's offer. He bought the store, had a going-out-of-business sale, and sold $12,000.00 worth of merchandise in about two weeks. He repaid the loan and re-opened as *Howard's*.

The Miskelly retail legacy was born.

Now that Howard and Ann were settled in Okolona, another little girl, Marty, joined the family. A spiritual heritage was important to both Howard and Ann, so they had to decide how they were going to raise their children and choose a church. Howard was raised Baptist and Ann was Methodist, but they knew they had to commit to one of them for the sake of their little family.

"Ann," said Howard, "we need to make a decision. We can't keep dragging these children back and forth between two churches. Now one of us is going to have to give here."

Ann looked at him with a calm resolve. "Hmm," she said. "I bet I know which one of us it's going to be." And with that, they joined the Baptist church. Howard did make her a deal, though. If they ever moved to a new town, Ann would get to choose the church.

Howard's stayed in that location for five years, and business was booming. It grew a little bit every year, and people responded to their selection and their integrity with their dollars and their loyalty.

Besides, Howard and Ann were a great combination. Howard had become well-versed in the area of men's clothing, but he knew absolutely nothing about women's. Ann, though, had a natural gift for it. She instinctively knew what to buy and stock, and she knew what their customers wanted and needed. Both of them had grown up around businesses, so they were naturals. And it worked. With each of them at home in their own area of expertise, *Howard's* was soon in need of more room.

The store that they had bought from Mr. Gordon was twenty-five feet wide and sixty feet long, and they were using every inch of it. After five years of business, the woman who owned the store next door approached them. She was a fine Jewish lady who owned a well-loved department store named *Rubel's*. But, much like Mr. Gordon, she was getting older. She was the last living member of the large family that had started *Rubel's*, and now she just wanted to sell it. Her store was two stories, fifty-five feet wide and one hundred fifty-five feet long, more than twice the size of Howard's. Once again, Howard and Ann talked and prayed, and together they decided that it was too good to pass up. He paid her $50,000, moved in and sold about $80,000 in the first ten days. So, they kept the original store and *Howard's* was suddenly triple the size that it was before. And the people kept coming.

Saturday nights were always a big deal in Okolona. Howard's stayed open until 10 pm, and it was necessary to accommodate all the people. Okolona was a farming community, and most of the farmers had about five families of African-Americans who lived on their farms and worked for them. On Saturday evenings, those farmers would bring all of their employees to town so that they could shop. The town square of Okolona was so crowded from six to ten pm on Saturday that you could hardly walk through it on the sidewalk.

Even though it was Mississippi in the early 1950s, Howard and Ann Miskelly had nothing but love and respect for their black friends and neighbors. They were wonderful customers, and they always tried hard to pay their credit bills on time. Ann remembers that there was a cultural anomaly in that black community--when they came in to buy shoes, no matter how big their feet were, the women would always say they wore a size 7. They would buy that 7, squeeze their feet into them, and walk out with their head held high.

During one particular fashion phase, the popular shoe was a ballerina shoe with a strap across the front. Ann, however, had to learn that that's what some of her customers were looking for when they requested a "bamaroona with a strop." *Howard's* sold hundreds and hundreds of pairs of shoes in those years for $2.98 a pair. Their profit on each pair was a dollar.

For the next 40 years, *Howard's* never had a bad year. For Howard and Ann, it was clear that their success had come from the Lord, and they thanked him every day.

Howard's best friend in those days was a young man named Harvey Fisher. Harvey was even taller than Howard, towering over him at 6'7". Howard and Harvey hit it off right away, and they saw each other often, because Harvey's father owned the store on the other side of *Gordon's*, which would soon become *Howard's*. Harvey eventually took over his father's store, and for years, Harvey and Howard met every day at 10 a.m. and 2 p.m. in Howard's store for coffee and good conversation. To this day, they are still best friends.

Chapter 11
Open for Business

Running a family business was, in fact, a family business. Everyone was put to work. The Miskelly children grew up knowing what it meant to work in a clothing store, and Howard's was the better for it. While living in Okolona, the Miskelly family had been completely rounded out with a total of five children: two girls (Pam and Marty) and three boys (Chip, Oscar, and Tommy). Ann had also taken on a nickname, and she was known as "Meme" by almost everyone, including her children. From the time they were tall enough to reach the counter, Meme had them wrapping boxes. In fact, at Christmas time, people would come and shop at Howard's just because they knew that the gifts from there would be the prettiest ones under the tree.

When the children were not working at the store,

they were under the keen and watchful eye of Levada Moore Lawson. After a short succession of housekeepers, they found their treasure in the woman known simply as "Vada". Even through the turbulent 1950s and 1960s of rural Mississippi, Vada was more than a housekeeper, she was family. The kids loved her fiercely, and she loved them the same way. Her husband, Jack, was the chauffeur for the richest man in town, a shrewd but likeable Jewish businessman named E.E. Davis, but everyone in town just called him "Mister".

Vada and Jack had eight children of their own, but there was always one of them old enough to watch the others as she left early in the morning to arrive at the Miskelly home before the family started stirring. Her greeting to Howard was the same every day: "Mr. Howard, are you gonna git up today?"

Howard's store was just one in the shopping district of downtown Okolona, and just like in most smaller towns, the store owners all supported one another. In fact, they needed each other. The retail business is symbiotic. One store only survives if other stores around it whose products are interdependent also thrive. Thus, many lifelong friendships are formed in the business neighborhood.

Every morning, without fail, a group of men met in the back of Howard's at 9:30 sharp for coffee and conversation. This daily meeting became a staple of life for them. Friendships were birthed and strengthened, and over the years, they walked with each other through the storms and sunny days. But, no matter what any of them were going through, the conversation eventually turned to Mississippi State football.

Howard and his friends kept up-to-date on the best high school athletes around the entire region, and how they might be recruited to play for State. This group of armchair coaches grew and matured in their scouting abilities, and over time, the back room at Howard's became the envy of college coaches and scouts everywhere. It was common for the men of Howard's coffee klatch to have huge pictures of the potential stars pinned up across the room, complete with stats and records attached. The men would argue, examine, compare, and decide among themselves who would be the best recruits. They had a fantasy football team for Mississippi State decades before there was even such a thing as fantasy football.

Those days and skills served Howard well, though. Today, in one corner of the south end zone of Davis Wade Stadium at Mississippi State University's Scott Field, resides the plush and impressive *Howard L. Miskelly, Sr. Recruiting Center*, replete with a large oil portrait of Howard Miskelly displayed front and center. When Howard walks on campus, all of the young recruits recognize him. Their predecessors, whose pictures and stats hung in the back room of Howard's all those years ago would be proud. Just by their presence, they helped inspire Howard's vision, and they paved the way for many of the football careers now being played out on the hallowed turf of Mississippi State University.

One night, saving the family business became a family business, too. Late in the evening, the Miskelly's phone rang and Howard took a frantic call.

"Howard!" the caller said, "you've got to get down to the store right now! The store across the street is on fire, and the wind is blowing your way!"

Howard wasted no time, dressing in a hurry and dashing out the door. The whole family was instantly on alert, and they all rushed to the store as one. Sure enough, a fire was raging from the store directly across the street from Howard's, and the flames were licking the night, as if they were reaching for the clothing store that was just out of reach. As the firefighters engaged the inferno across the street, Howard rushed to the roof of his own building with a bucket brigade right behind him. For what seemed like all night, Howard and his family doused the roof of his store, one bucket after another, after another, until the threatening blaze was out. Afterward, exhausted and shaking, everyone agreed that it was that continuous flow of water across the top of the building that made it possible for *Howard's* to avoid the talons of disaster and open, undamaged, the following morning.

Chapter 12
Better or Worse

Birthdays in the Miskelly household have always been celebrated with great love and attention. One particular year, for Ann's birthday, Howard arranged for the two of them to go out to dinner with friends in her honor. That evening, four other couples arrived at the Miskelly home to caravan to a favorite restaurant that was about forty-five minutes away.

Everyone was walking out of the house and getting into their respective automobiles when Ann realized that she had left her purse in the house. She quietly turned around and went back inside to get it.

Howard slid behind the wheel of his car and noticed that Ann wasn't with him. She had been right behind him, so he figured she had gotten caught up in conversation and had decided to ride with one of their friends in order to continue it. He pulled out of the driveway and down the street, along with the others.

Just as they turned the corner and pulled out of sight, Ann emerged from their house, purse in hand. Everyone was gone. *Okay,* she thought, *that's a good joke. Leave me behind on my birthday dinner. Very funny.* She knew they would be back around the corner in just a moment, and they would all have a good laugh.

A few miles out of town, Howard pulled up next to one of the other couples at a stoplight. They looked over and noticed that Ann wasn't with him, so they guessed she must have ridden with someone else. Howard smiled and waved. The light turned green.

Ann stood alone on the front porch for more than a few minutes. Eventually, she knew she had been forgotten. She looked in her purse for the house key so that she could at least go inside and wait for them to realize the mistake and come back for her. The key wasn't in there. Howard had it. She had locked herself out of the house. Calmly, but with steam in her step, she walked around the back of the house, found a brick, and threw it through the glass on the kitchen door. She reached through the jagged opening, felt for the lock, turned it, and opened the door. She was getting madder by the moment.

Ann's friends and husband arrived at the designated restaurant and gathered in the lobby. "Howard," said one of the women, "where's Ann?"

"What do you mean?" said Howard.

"Where's Ann?" she repeated. "Didn't she ride with you?"

"Well, no," said Howard, "I thought she rode with you."

"Not us," she said. They looked around. "Did any of you bring Ann with you?"

No one had. It dawned on Howard. "Uh-oh," he said. But, since they had driven forty-five minutes to get here, there wasn't time to go back. So, they sat down at their table and ate Ann's birthday dinner.

Howard pulled into the driveway and noticed that all of the lights were out. When he walked to the back door and saw the broken glass and the brick on the kitchen floor, he knew he was in trouble. He walked upstairs and quietly put on his pajamas so as not to awaken his sleeping wife. Just as he touched the sheets and began to slide in next to her, he heard a terrifying voice from the darkness: "Don't you even think about setting one foot in this bed."

He didn't argue. He had no defense. Howard gently took his pillow and headed obediently down the hall to the guest bedroom.

Eventually, Ann came to him and said, "Alright, Howard, I'm not mad anymore. You can come back to our room."

But it was a good three days later.

❦

Everyone involved in a retail business must, by necessity, keep up with developments in their industry, but nowhere is this seen more keenly than in the world of fashion. Swiftly changing styles and ever-evolving tastes of customers require that retailers be up-to-date on what is new and what will be selling next season. Howard and Ann knew that to be true, so to that end, they attended a regional trade show twice a year, alternating between Dallas and Memphis.

There were always multi-day events that were time well spent for the young couple as they sought to keep their Okolona clothing store flying high. Hundreds of clothiers would meet at these shows and map out their buying strategy for the coming year. After a few days of work, the last night was a party. A ballroom was rented, food and drink were served, music played, and a good time was had by all. Well, almost all.

Howard and Ann had arrived at the ball, happy with their work and ready to enjoy the evening. Howard, always gregarious and not very shy, made friends wherever he found people. As the evening went on, he found himself enjoying the company of two particular young women who couldn't get enough of his stories, wit, and charm.

Ann was sitting at a table by herself as Howard sat at another table, regaling the girls with whatever made them laugh. As she sat, she began to fume. As she fumed, a young man who was a friend of Howard and Ann's came over and said, only half-jokingly into her ear, "Hey, Ann, you better look out, there. Looks like Howard's got quite a fan club going." Then he walked away.

Ann had sat and watched long enough. She took a breath, stood, smoothed her dress, and with great sophistication, picked up a nearby pitcher of ice water. She walked over to the table where Howard sat with a girl on each side, his arms on the backs of their chairs, all three of them laughing at some story, as a long Roi-Tan cigar dangled rakishly from his lips. Without a word, Ann stood in front of Howard and poured the entire pitcher of frigid water over his head. Like an actor in a classic movie, Howard didn't move a muscle. He didn't dodge out of the way, nor did he jump up, mad and wet. He just sat there, as the water cascaded over him, dousing both his cigar and his sense of adventure.

Ann, satisfied, set down the pitcher and walked away. As she did, Howard looked at the two young girls beside him, and said, with what seemed like genuine innocence, "Who was that woman?"

He might have played it coy, but he also didn't stay sitting at that table any longer.

Chapter 13
Life With Father

Running a successful business afforded Howard and Meme (Ann) a few luxuries from time to time, including the opportunity to travel. But, just like any other couple with children still at home, arrangements needed to be made in order to ensure that everyone was safe and sound while they were gone.

One particular year, Howard and Meme took a two-week trip to Europe. Howard, of course, had practically walked across Europe some years before as a soldier, but Meme had never been, and this gave him a chance to show her the beauty of it without either of them worrying about being engaged in mortal combat. By this time, Tommy, their youngest, was sixteen years old, which was, in Howard's estimation, old enough to care for himself, but Vada would still be around during the day, and Oscar would probably come home from college on the weekend.

Tommy could, of course, fend for himself, but that didn't keep him from being a little nervous at night, all by himself in the house. Before he went to sleep, Tommy barricaded himself in Howard and Meme's bedroom, since it felt the most secure and fortress-like. He locked the bedroom door, loaded the family shotgun, propped it against the wall in arm's reach, and crawled into his parents' bed and waited for morning.

On Friday of the first week, Tommy relaxed a little. He knew Oscar would be home for the next couple of nights, and on Friday evening, he went out with friends. While he was gone, Oscar arrived home, ate supper, and looked around the house. He went into Howard and Meme's room, where Tommy had been holed up, and examined the setup. Oscar shook his head and laughed a little at Tommy's insecurity. He walked around the room, straightened the bedcovers a little, and sat down. He looked to his left and noticed the shotgun leaning against the wall near the bed. *Sheesh, Tommy,* he thought, *how in the world can an empty shotgun make you feel safer?* Oscar stood, walked over, and picked up the shotgun. It felt good in his hands. He looked at himself in the full length mirror. It not only felt good, it looked good on him, too. Oscar had seen lots of Clint Eastwood movies, and he wondered how good he would be in one of those scenes. *Pretty good,* he reckoned. Imitating what he had seen, Oscar held the gun hip level, swung around quickly toward an imaginary enemy, and pulled the trigger.

BOOM!

The ear-splitting noise made Oscar yell in shock, and the recoil made his hands go numb for a moment. He looked in the direction of the two barrels, and saw that he had blown a gaping hole right through the side of the house in his mother and father's bedroom. *Oh, no!* he thought. *I just killed somebody! If there was someone on the other side of that wall, I just killed them!*

Oscar dropped the gun, bolted out the front door, and ran to the side of the house to see who might be laid out there. He skidded to a stop. The yard was empty. There had been no one there. He thought for a moment about the phrase "dodging a bullet," until he looked up and realized that he could see right into his parents' bedroom. The thin siding, along with the insulation and the inside sheetrock, had been blasted away.

When Tommy arrived home later that evening, his mouth fell open at the sight. "Oscar!" he said, "what did you do?"

"Well for crying out loud, Tommy!" said Oscar. "Why in the world would you leave a loaded shotgun leaning against the wall? I never thought it would have something in it!"

"You know Mom and Dad are going to kill you."

"Not if I can help it," said Oscar, with a good amount of resolve. "They're gone for another week. I can fix it."

He felt pretty good about his chances until Vada came to work the next morning and saw the damage. "Good Lord!" she screamed. "Oscar! What in the world you done?!?"

"Now Vada," said Oscar, "I'm gonna fix it. But you can't ever tell Howard and Meme about this. You understand, Vada? Never! You promise me?"

"Alright, Oscar," said Vada, "I promise. But you sure nuff better fix it good." Vada walked away, shaking her head, muttering "Lord, Lord, Lord," just loud enough for Oscar to hear her.

The next day, Oscar made a trip to the local hardware store. "Hey, Al," he said to the proprieter, a family friend. "Listen, some of the boys at the dorm were horsing around, and one of them put a hole in one of the walls. What would I need to get to fix that?"

His friend walked him around the store and showed him the materials required. Oscar made the purchase, charging it to Howard, of course, and loaded up his car with mud, spreaders, sheetrock, siding, and whatever else he was told that he needed. Immediately, he went to work patching the hole in the house.

Oscar worked tirelessly for the next four or five days, often staying up all night to get it done before going to class the next day. He sawed, he spackled, he mudded, he sanded, he painted. Night after sleepless night. Finally, he matched the interior bedroom paint color as closely as he could and painted over the repair. He finished the job, and with not a moment to spare. Howard and Meme would be home in less than 36 hours, and it was just enough time for everything inside and outside to dry.

Upon declaring the project a success as the morning sun began to brighten in the windows, his eyes growing heavier every second, Oscar took the paint brushes, trays, and spreaders to the utility room to wash them out. He put them in the large sink and turned on the faucet so that they could soak under the running water for a few minutes. Then he went into the living room and sat down on the couch to rest for a second, while the sink filled.

Suddenly, Oscar was being shaken by someone. "Oscar!" he heard them say. "Oscar! Get yourself up!" He recognized Vada's voice, but she hadn't been there just a moment ago. He looked at his watch. In an instant, he knew that he had fallen asleep without knowing it. An hour had passed. He swung his feet off the couch and heard a very disconcerting splash. Oscar looked down. The living room carpet was submerged in three inches of water.

Vada was splashing into the utility room. "Why you left the water on, Oscar?!? Now just look what you done!"

Howard and Meme were coming home tomorrow. There was only one thing to do. Oscar grabbed the phone and the phone book, looked up the closest carpet cleaning company, and called them out to the house right away, again charging it to Howard. *Hey, Mom and Dad!* he figured he would say. *I got the carpets cleaned for you as a welcome home surprise!*

A few days after their uneventful return from Europe, Howard and Meme were lying in bed just before turning out the lights and going to sleep. Meme frowned at one part of the wall. "Howard," she said, "does that look right to you?"

"Does what look right?" he said.

"Right over there." She pointed. "Does that paint look a little bit different than the rest of the room to you?"

Howard squinted at the wall. "I suppose it does," he said. "I guess I've just never noticed it before. Good night, honey," he said. And he rolled over and closed his eyes.

"Hmm," said Meme, still looking at the wall. "Good night." She kept the light on and looked at the wall another minute. "Hmm," she said again.

The next morning, Howard and Meme were in the kitchen for breakfast as Vada was busying herself with the morning chores. "Hey, Vada," said Meme. "Did anything happen while we were gone?"

Vada slowed down perceptibly and her eyes widened. "Uh, no ma'am, Miss Meme, ain't nothing happened."

She kept working, but she knew that Meme was on to her.

"Now, Vada," Meme said, "I'm going to ask you again. "Did anything happen while we were gone?" Vada tried to keep her promise to Oscar, but she couldn't help it now. To her great surprise, the whole story came rolling out, peppered with her infectious laughter.

By the time Oscar came home from college again, the secret was out, and Howard and Meme were not mad anymore. In fact, Howard was pretty impressed with Oscar's workmanship on the wall. No one was hurt and everything was restored to normal.

But Oscar never had access to the shotgun again.

Howard Miskelly had three basic rules for raising children:

1. Take them to Sunday School and church every Sunday.

2. Make them work.

3. Don't give them a lot of money, even when they're in college.

Howard was a firm believer that children should grow in responsibility through real life lessons, especially when it came to money. Sometimes those lessons were learned the hard way.

Tommy was the youngest of the five Miskelly children, and by the time he was sixteen, Howard and Ann had achieved a nice amount of success in business. Now at driving age, Tommy was itching to own a car, and he knew that his dad could make that happen for him without much effort. Tommy was working in the family business, so he had a pretty good regular income for a high school student, but he was hoping that he wouldn't have to use any of his hard-earned money for the car.

"Hey, Dad," he said, "I'm thinking about buying a car. What do you think?"

"Well," said Howard, "how much money do you have?"

"Enough," said Tommy, "at least for a down payment."

"I don't know, son," said Howard, "do you really want to have a car payment? Don't you want to buy something outright?"

"Well," said Tommy, "I want to get something a good bit nicer than what I can pay cash for."

"Well," said Howard, "it's your money. If you want to go look around at the car lot that my friend Cookie Epperson owns, I'll go with you. Me and Cookie will get you fixed up."

That's it! thought Tommy. *"I'll go with you."* Surely *that means he is going to help with the down payment. He might even just buy the car for me!*

Together, Tommy and Howard went down to the lot, and Tommy looked around. In short order, he found the perfect car. Sleek. Powerful. Shiny. Perfect. "This is the one," said Tommy. "I'm sure of it."

"Okay," said Howard, "let's go in and talk to Cookie." Tommy could hardly contain himself. They went inside, Howard introduced his son, and said, "Cookie, Tommy wants this car. Can you set him up?"

"Sure thing," said Cookie. "Sit down right here, Tommy." Tommy sat at a gunmetal gray desk as Cookie went over the numbers with him. He showed him how much he needed to put down, how taxes and registration figured in, and how much he would be paying per month. It was at this point that Tommy expected Howard to chime in with his offer to pay.

Nothing.

Tommy looked over his shoulder. Howard wasn't there. He was out on the lot, browsing. Kicking tires. Reading price stickers. Looking in windows.

Tommy was on his own.

Over the next few minutes, as Tommy and Cookie talked, it became clear that he could not afford the perfect car that he had picked out. Back out on the lot they went, and Tommy finally settled on a 1981 cream colored Oldsmobile Cutlass Supreme. Back inside with Cookie, Tommy walked, all by himself, through the contracts and credit reports, and, all by himself, he counted out the money he needed to pay to take the car home. Cookie handed him the keys, congratulated him on his fine purchase, and opened the door for him to slide behind the wheel. Howard smiled at him, waved, and got into his own car to head home.

Tommy learned a lasting lesson that day. He knew that his father would always be there for him, would never turn him away, and would always be willing to help if help was needed. But today wasn't about needing help. Today was about choices. Tommy had made his. And he would never forget it.

⚜

It wasn't too long after, when another life lesson made an indelible impression on Tommy. Winter had come, and in north Mississippi, you could expect a wintry mix of snow, ice, and freezing rains at least a few times each season. One of those storms had hit, but to Tommy, the weather was just a small inconvenience. He wanted to go somewhere, and he had a car, so he was going.

Howard saw Tommy preparing to leave, so he advised him. "Tommy," he said, "you don't want to go nowhere in this weather. Those roads are awful slick."

"I'll be alright," Tommy tossed back.

"Now, Tommy," said Howard, "you haven't been driving that long, and you don't know what it's like to drive on ice. You have no control. You need to stay home."

Tommy, though, in stereotypical teenager fashion, would have none of it. "Dad!" he said. "Leave me alone! I know what I'm doing. I can drive!"

Howard relented, but not out of defeat. It was more of the resolve of age and wisdom. "Alright," he said, "if you're sure."

Tommy marched out the house, got in his car, revved the engine, and backed out of the drive.

It was about five minutes later that the Miskelly's phone rang. It was the police. "Hello, Howard," said the officer, "just thought I'd let you know about something."

"What's that?" said Howard.

"Well, it seems that your boy, Tommy, just slid all the way down your street. He's done broadsided a Cadillac."

No one was hurt, but another life lesson was tattooed on Tommy's heart: sometimes, in fact, father really does know best. There was another incident, though, when Howard demonstrated to Tommy the vast difference between justice and grace.

Tommy and a few of his friends were killing a Friday night by gently aggravating some girls with whom they attended high school. The girls were by themselves for the evening at one of their homes, the daughter of a prominent Okolona resident. The boys spent a little while ringing the doorbell and running away, and other assorted harmless pranks that made the girls roll their eyes and giggle.

After a while, though, as boys are prone to do, they found themselves discovering a dead possum. Of course, the next step was obvious. They took the dead possum, placed it on the front doorstep, and rang the bell and ran again. The girls came out, saw the carcass, and screamed hysterically. The prominent man's daughter was so distraught that she called her father and alerted him to the situation. The boys, with a sense that they had gotten in over their heads, scattered and headed to their own houses.

The father, not one to take a joke easily, jumped in his car and peeled out of his office parking lot to rush home and save his daughter from the deceased marsupial. He then proceeded to hunt down every one of the boys involved, speed to their house, and let them have whatever piece of his mind he felt he could spare. In just at little while, he was banging on Howard Miskelly's front door.

"Hello," said Howard, " opening the door. "How can

I help you tonight?"

"You can't help me," he yelled, "but maybe I can help you!" He stubbed out one cigarette and lit another, his face as red as the flame that now glowed at the end of it. "I think you have a little hoodlum right there," he said, pointing to Tommy, who was shaking in his sneakers across the room. "Maybe I can help you keep him out of jail! That boy right there and his friends just scared my little girl half to death with their pranks! Left a dead possum right there on my doorstep! Now, Howard, I'm going to leave this in your hands for now, and I hope you will take care of business, because if it happens again, I'll come down here and do it myself!" he stormed off the porch, got in his car, slammed the door, and the tires spit gravel leaving the house. Howard hadn't said a word.

Tommy knew he had it coming now. No way he was talking his way out of this one. He had obviously embarrassed himself and Howard, and he was already calculating what his punishment might be. Howard turned toward him and shook his head.

"Good Lord," said Howard, "that man needs to calm down. He's gonna give himself a heart attack." He walked past Tommy, patting him on the shoulder. And that was it. Tommy had never felt the urge to be a good man more than he did at that moment. He realized in an instant the power of grace. When justice was needed, Howard could certainly give it. But when he stood in your corner, there was no safer place to be. And Tommy knew that he wanted to honor that kind of love for the rest of his life.

⚜

As a respected business man in Okolona, Howard was proud to be part of a team that secured government funding for the establishment of the Okolona Country Club. The other man on that team was Howard's long time and close friend, Ted Casey. Together, Howard and Ted founded the brand new facility, complete with a beautiful, professionally designed golf course, a swinmming pool, and tennis courts. One evening, the whole family was out, enjoying the new club, and Howard was playing tennis on the lighted courts when some of his children came running to him in a panic.

"Dad! Dad! Come quick!" Howard let the ball go by and moved toward them.

"What is it?" he said. "What's wrong?"

"It's Oscar! He fell off the high dive!"

Howard ran with his children to the other side of the complex, where the beautiful, blue-water pool had been built. At one end of the pool was a diving board that reached almost thirty feet up. Laying crumpled on the concrete at the base of the ladder was 12-year-old Oscar. "What happened?" asked Howard as he ran to him.

"We don't know, he just fell! We thought he might hit the water, but he didn't."

Oscar was unconscious. Howard picked him up and ran to the car. Howard's tennis partner that night was a local doctor and family friend, so he followed close behind.

Friends and family gathered at the hospital waiting room over the next few minutes and hours. No one knew what to expect, but they were not optimistic. Oscar had fallen from such a tremendous height, almost three stories, onto concrete. It didn't look good. The gash in Oscar's head was such that Howard could see the stark white of his skull.

But, Howard and Ann, as full of faith as ever, asked people to pray for Oscar. So, all through the night, both in the hospital and over phone lines from house to house, the people of Okolona prayed for Oscar. And as they waited, Howard encouraged everyone there, even the doctors and nurses, to believe that God was good, and that He would demonstrate that goodness that very night. Whomever he talked to, Howard encouraged everyone to place their trust firmly in the hands of a loving God.

And in the morning, as dawn snuck in around the edges of the blinds in Oscar's hospital room, Oscar woke up. Within about an hour, he was discharged, patched up nicely, with no lasting injury. The Miskelly family had been raised to believe that prayer works and that God heals. And now they had seen it firsthand for themselves, and they would never forget this night.

The Miskelly family's popular clothing store became a fixture of downtown Okolona, and it was an important piece of the community. Howard had always been a man of service, so he sought out ways to make connections and friendships that helped tie his community together. He even ran for mayor once. He lost it in the runoff, and though Howard shrugged off the loss, his oldest daughter, Pam, cried for three days. Howard knew it was for the best, though. At that time you couldn't be mayor and own a business, and Howard was not going to lose his business for that.

Howard was proud of his friendships throughout the county, and it was with great satisfaction that he often helped someone by getting them out of a traffic ticket. With the declaration that he would "take care of it," Howard would then make a call to a friend on the police force and do just that.

One day, the nephew of a friend received a speeding ticket in the southern part of the county, and he called Howard. "Hey, Mr. Howard," said the young man, "I know you have some connections, and I was wondering if you could help me out with this ticket?"

Howard had to think about that one, because he didn't have any connections in that part of the county. "Sure," he said, "just bring it to me. I'll take care of it."

Chip was with him when he made that promise, and he knew his dad was at something of a loss, but he figured that Howard must know someone that he didn't.

After a couple of weeks, just in passing conversation, Chip asked him about it. "Hey, Dad," he said, "I didn't know that you had connections with the police in the southern part of the county."

"I don't," said Howard.

"But you took care of that guy's ticket, right?"

"Yes, I did."

"Then how did you do that?"

Howard shrugged. "I paid it."

Howard and Ann's parenting skills produced five God-loving, responsible adults, but it also prepared their children to be good husbands and wives. As the five children grew into marrying age, those new in-laws sometimes felt they had big shoes to fill. Howard, though, true to form, was never aloof or distant. He treated his children-in-law the same way that he treated his children-by-birth.

Pam, for instance, the oldest of the five, married a wonderful man named Chuck, and they had a good and strong marriage. Howard and Chuck hit it off well, and they treated each other with honesty and respect. One of Chuck's favorite memories was a phone conversation that he had with Howard.

"Hey Chuck," said Howard on answering the phone. "How are you?"

"Well, Howard," he said, "I've been better. Pam and I have had a pretty good argument. She is really mad, and to be honest, I don't know what to do. Any suggestions?" Chuck knew that Howard knew his daughter well, so he waited for the sage advice that would guide him down these rough waters. Howard's reply was simple.

"Yes," he said, "don't bring her over here."

⚜

When Tommy started dating Lisa, whom he would later marry, it was clear that they could have a real future together. Lisa had written Tommy a letter and playfully signed it "Mrs. Tommy Miskelly." It just so happened, though, that the letter only found its way to Tommy after Howard had mistakenly read it first.

Tommy soon invited Lisa over to their home for Thanksgiving to meet the family, and she gladly accepted. That Thursday morning, she tried on at least four different outfits. Then she tried them on again. Tommy picked her up, and as they pulled into the driveway, she could feel the fluttering of her stomach. Lisa was introduced all around, and everyone was very nice to her, but she was still nervous. She especially wanted to make a good impression on Howard.

After the dinner was eaten and the places were cleared, the boys went out front to toss the football around, while the women busied themselves with the finishing touches in the kitchen. Lisa walked over to the wall of windows that stretched across the back of the house in the living room and looked out on the serenity of the north Mississippi woods in the fall. Howard came up and stood next to her, admiring the scene with her. After a few moments, he spoke.

"I'm a lucky man," he said.

"Yes sir," said Lisa. "You certainly are. You have a lovely family."

Howard turned to her. "True," said Howard, "but that's not what I was talking about. I meant I'm a lucky man because I got to be with you today."

After 40 years of faithful service, *Howard's* closed its doors as its owners retired. The boys, now grown, were interested in opening clothing stores of their own, but Meme had a better idea. "That's not where the money is now," she said. "Look around at all of the furniture factories in north Mississippi. You boys could be more successful with a furniture store."

And so it was that Miskelly Furniture was born, with its flagship store in Pearl, Mississippi. *Miskelly Furniture* is now the largest furniture operation in the southeastern United States.

Chapter 14
Howard Miskelly, Friend and Mentor

Sometimes the best way to get a glimpse into the depth of a friendship is to hear it directly from the friends themselves. Following are the words of three of Howard's lifelong friends-- Celia Fisher, Claude Adams, and Raymond Osborne:

∽✦⊱

Harvey and Celia Fisher have been Howard and Meme's close friends for more than 50 years. Celia sums up that deep friendship here:

One never knows the great friendships that will develop in life. In 1952, Harvey and I were young teenagers in Okolona just finishing the ninth and sixth grades respectively. A young couple with three children (later there would be five) moved to town to open a department store. Howard and Ann Miskelly immediately became involved in their new community, church, school and civic organizations. For example, Howard started the practice of letting the seniors at Okolona High School run the store for a day. I even wrapped packages there at Christmas and learned not to waste paper or ribbon. Maybe he was preaching conservatism even then.

Three years after the Miskellys moved to town, Harvey enrolled at Mississippi State. That of course could only improve Howard's opinion of him. Ten years after Ann and Howard moved to Okolona, we Fishers and our little daughter (there would later be two more) returned to Okolona to live after two years at Fort Sill, Oklahoma. We were adults then and Fisher Hardware and Furniture was located right next door to Howard's Department Store. Thus began a relationship that has stood the test of time. Every day, twice a day, the two men met in the "coffee room" in the back of Howard's store. I've actually seen a little resentment in their expressions when any of us intruded on their discussions. This also started another practice that continued until the Miskellys sold the store in 1992. Every year on "Signing Day", Howard and Harvey hung a big poster board listing all that year's signees for both Mississippi State and Ole Miss. It included name, position, height and weight. If a player left the team for any reason, a big red line was drawn through their name. Coach Jackie Sherill was very upset with Howard when he did not save those posters when he sold the store. There is no telling the number of times the two men loaded up and went to Starkville to watch practice or how many basketball games they attended, even in the old Babe McCarthy Gym. Of course they got tickets together at the new "Hump". They even included Ann and me. How many ball game trips we made to Starkville, Jackson and other places each fall!

Howard and Harvey had much more in common than Mississippi State and football. When the Okolona Country Club was organized they were charter members. Every Wednesday afternoon and most Sunday afternoons for over forty years they played golf together. We two couples belonged to a supper club with other couples that lasted nearly forty years. Ann and I belonged to the same bridge club. I taught all five Miskelly children World and American History at Okolona High School and always knew I had the backing of their parents.

It is easy to see why I say it saddened us when Howard and Ann made the decision to leave Okolona and move to Old Waverly. But that's only thirty miles away and we still enjoy visits with our dear friends of many years.

Claude Adams was a young African-American man from Okolona when he met Howard in the store while shopping with his mother. A friendship was struck, and Howard became Claude's mentor, a relationship which has lasted for more than 35 years.

I lived in Okolona, went to school in Okolona, and he had a clothing store. My Mom used to go in there, and he was always a loving man, a loving person. It was about 1979, I was 15 years old. I lived in the country a few miles from Okolona. I used to go to his house for Bible study after school. I had fell on hard times through life, and a lot of people gave up on me, even family members gave up on me, but I always could count on him mentoring and ministering to me in my life. He has been a big influence in my family life, and I've met so many people great people through him. He has been just like Jesus Christ to me. He has been a friend, a father figure, he's been everything a person ever could be in my life, and I just love him for it. He has been there for me through thick and thin, through the good times and bad times. He's the kind of man that I want to live like and my children to be like. He has a great passion for people, a great passion for Jesus Christ. He won me to Christ.

For a long time, I would go to his house and we used to watch football games, and there would be somebody in the stands holding up this sign that said, "3:16." And the clock would get past 3:16, and I was always wondering about that. So, I asked him what that meant, and he opened the Bible and said, "No, that's a scripture in the Bible. Here, I'm going to show you this right here." And he turned to John 3:16: "For God so loved the world, that he gave His only begotten Son, that whosoever believes in Him shall not perish, but have everlasting life."

I asked him, "What does that mean?" I had no idea. We laughed about it later, but it was the greatest thing he had ever showed me. I didn't understand much of anything about the Bible. I couldn't read very well, but right there, he took time out and prayed with me and showed me how to believe in the Lord and the Scriptures. I can't say enough, he's just wonderful, and probably, him not being in my life, there's no telling what my life would be. Howard put me on the right path in life. He could have chosen someone else, he could have turned away from me. But he's been with me through the dark times of life-- in and out of jail, prison, alcohol and drugs. He has been the driving force for me not to give up. I just love him and am thankful for him. He has been everything that anyone would ever need in their life.

Howard is loved by so many people, he is a blessing. I don't know if he ever told me "No," and if he did, it was for the best reason, a right reason. He has done more for me than he has done for his own children and grandkids. And he is still in my life, no matter what it is, I know the good Lord put him in my life, because he has really saved my life, he has really turned it around. We go way back.

I can remember the first day meeting him, it was like a match made in heaven, we just took off, and we been taking off ever since. We've been down some rough roads, but things have come to an end, and my life is not done. I have wavered and fought in my Christian walk, but Howard never gave up. He talked to me about changing, and living for Christ. As I got older, and matured, and got my life in shape, everywhere I go, I give testimony, and Howard comes to the front of the story. He has been a driving force for me.

I could write a book about our relationship, but the best thing about it, he led me to Christ. Couldn't nobody else do it, my Mom, Granddaddy, Grandmama tried to do it, and I just never would buy into it, but sometimes the Lord picks people that are not of the same race or whatever they may be, and he has been the one who's been able to do it. It's not been an easy job for him, and he would probably tell you that. But he's been there.

I got a chance to meet so many people through him-- coaches, players, business people, ministers. We went to church together, fellowshipped together, Bible study. Then I was able to teach other people what he was teaching me. I got the inspiration from him. I got the gift from him, and I give the Lord all the credit, because that's where it all came from. He would talk to me about the Lord, and I didn't get a lot of that at home. I came from a poor family, we didn't have running water. But

Mr. Howard, he gave me clothes, helped me get to school. I didn't have a father, and he was like a father to me. He was everything to me.

My life has been blessed, and it started with Mr. Howard Miskelly, all those years ago, there on Main Street in Okolona, Mississippi.

Raymond Osborne began working at Howard's as a teenager, and he has modeled his life after Howard, or "Big H," as he calls him, ever since. Like Claude Adams, Raymond was an African-American teenager in Mississippi in a volatile era, but all he ever experienced from Howard Miskelly was acceptance and opportunity.

We met in the spring of 1972. I was 16 years old. I met Howard through his son, Oscar. I had always wanted to work at their store, so one day at school, I asked Oscar if he could ask his Dad if he needed any help at the store, because I needed a job. Oscar went and talked to him and came back to school and said for me to go see his Dad. Back then they called it cooperative education. I would go to school half a day and then go to work at Howard's for the rest of the day.

The first thing I learned from Howard was how to take care of customers, having a genuine concern for them and giving them 100% good service. Then I learned the basics of working a job, too, punctuality, doing a very good job. The whole time with him was a great exposure to the retail business. He was a true mentor in getting me into that world.

He has also mentored me in being a good father, a good husband. He exemplified good, positive Christian values, and I still treasure those values to this day. He shared good instruction with his children as well as me. I was blessed to have good Christian parents, but having a second set there in Mr. and Mrs. Miskelly just fortified me.

Howard has always been there for me, all throughout the years. He always encouraged me to think outside the box. One time, he was going to be gone to a Mississippi State game, and he left a bunch of suits on sale for me to get rid of. He showed me the suits and said, "Now Raymond, this time around, these particular suits are going to be cash only. No layaways, no charges, strictly cash. I need to get these suits sold."

Well, at this time, in the mid-1970's, gospel singing was really getting big, especially in the African-American community. I had talked to some of my friends, and so I said, "Hey guys, y'all are my friends, and I sure would love for you to come by Howard's department store in Okolona, come down and look at some suits. And it just so happened that one of the singing groups came in that weekend, about eight or nine of them. They picked out suits, and fortunately, we had everybody's sizes. They would have to come back in a couple of days to pay for them, so I took those suits back to where we normally kept layaways, and we had a pullout rack. So I refreshed that rack and put the suits on the empty side of it.

Well, "Big H" (that's what I call him), he returns that Monday, and he asks the store manager, "Hey, what are these suits back here? There's a bunch of suits."

"I don't know," said the manager, "Raymond put them there this weekend."

So here I am coming into work from school, all happy, I had a good day at school. I saw him as I walked in. "Hey, Raymond," he said.

"Hey, how you doin', sir?"

"Looky here, quick question. I got some suits back there. Now, we had an understanding that there would be no layaways, no charges, strictly cash. Now what's going on with these suits?"

I said, "Well, these are on hangback. The customers are coming to get them." So I created a new department in the store, called "Hangback." So the guys came in that week and paid cash for the suits, and not only did we sell them the suits, they bought the shirts, ties, and from there we developed a good relationship with about eight or nine gospel quartets, and each of them ten or twelve guys per quartet. So we really did a phenomenal business on the suit side. And it was all because Howard taught me and trusted me to think outside the box and get creative. He gave me the confidence to know that I wasn't going to be in trouble for it, and it paid off in lots of ways.

I still work for the Miskellys, as part of the biggest furniture operation in the whole southeast. Those same principles, I apply today. I treat the customer with kindness and respect, and let them know that they are the one that makes everything possible for us. One of the things he instilled in me is being honest with the customer and telling them what's right. It has made me as successful as I am today, to remember to be honest with your customers, don't try to pull no fast ones.

At age 16, Howard took me in and made me a part of the family. You know, we are Mississippi State folks, and we are always trying to get one in on the Ole Miss folks. Well, they may have *"The Blind Side"* story, but I told Howard, "You know, they don't have anything on us. We are way ahead of them. Y'all had a black son way back in 1972!"

Chapter 15
Man of Bronze

One of the greatest joys of Howard Miskelly's life has been working with and on behalf of veterans in Mississippi. Largely because of Howard's work on the Mississippi State Veterans Affairs Board, Newton, Mississippi became the home of the Mississippi Veterans Memorial Cemetery, often referred to as "Arlington South." Veterans and their families have been able to choose the MVMC as a beautiful and majestic place of burial as an alternative to Arlington since 2011.

Another more personal tribute to Howard and his military service was revealed to the public on July 10, 2007. On that Tuesday morning, at the North Carolina International Furniture Market, brothers Ron and Todd Wanek presented the Miskelly family with a life-size bronze statue of Howard as a young man in uniform. As friends and members of the media gathered, Chip Miskelly, Howard and Meme's oldest son, stepped to the microphone and introduced special guests, including state and local officials, and US Army General Adjutant Harold Cross and his wife, Carolyn. "I told Harold," Chip said, "there are only about 20 or 30 people from Falkner, and you and Howard are two of them!"

Oscar then came up and introduced Ron and Todd Wanek, the founders and Chief Executive Officers of Ashley Furniture. The Waneks have been family friends for many years, and it was, in fact, Ron Wanek, who sculpted the bronze statue being unveiled. "Some years ago," said Ron Wanek, "I talked with Chip about the Soldier's Walk in Arcadia. Wisconsin. Soldier's Walk is a time walk, it's 500 meters long and along its time walk are various statues for all of the major wars and conflicts involving the United States. Many of them are done in the resemblances of the local soldiers in our area.

"Chip said to me, 'You know, Howard was in World War II.' And I did not know that. So we kept talking about it, and I said, 'I would really like to do a bronze of Howard. Why don't you get me some pictures and let's see what we can do.' To do a bronze like this will generally take about a year to do. They are usually pretty tough to do because you've got to get them from all angles, and sometimes photographs don't exist from that era of one's life, so you have to kind of improvise, but I had some pretty good pictures that were provided to me by Chip and his brothers. I think he came out pretty good, in fact, I think I nailed him better than anyone that I've ever done, and I feel pretty good about this statue. I think it is a very good likeness of Howard when he was 18 or 19 years old, and we've been very proud to do this." Turning to Howard, he said, "Truly, you are part of the greatest generation. Congratulations Howard, and thank you for everything that you have done."

Chip spoke again, and asked Howard to step forward and say a few words. As he came, with Meme by his side, Chip said, "You know, we talk about Howard all the time, and we put him out in front, but you know the real backbone of the family is Meme, our Mom. She is a very special lady, she has five kids, thirteen grandkids, and three great grandkids, and she is loved by all of them. They say behind every great man is a great woman, and in this case, it is certainly true. This is a special time. We are very proud of our father. He was a war hero, and a man that has mentored us in a very special way. We appreciate the way they have both raised us.

As Chip handed Howard the microphone, the trumpeter began to play *America the Beautiful,* the sheet over the statue was slipped off, and the six foot two inch bronze Howard Miskelly smiled into the room, standing at ease, hands clasped firmly behind his back. The flesh and blood Howard spoke next.

"Thank you very much. There's two or three things

I haven't been able to figure out yet. One is, General Cross and I went to the same school. I ended up a Staff Sergeant, and he ended up a General. The other thing is, I'm very emotional about this, and Oscar said he'd give me a hundred dollars if I didn't cry. So y'all help me to keep laughing.

"The Waneks will never know how much I appreciate this, Ron and Todd, and if everybody in the United States was as patriotic as those two people, this would be a much better place to live. Thank you very much for doing this for me. I appreciate it, and I'll never forget it. Thank you again, and may God bless each of you."

The crowd joined in as the trumpeter sounded the notes of *God Bless America*, and there was almost a tangible feeling in the room that, in ways large and small, God had certainly blessed America with a man named Howard L. Miskelly.

Chapter 16
The Longest Shadow

Howard Miskelly has, indeed, cast a long shadow. He has been a hero to some, an inspiration to many, and an example to all. His wife and children honor him with their lives as well as their words, and he has been a spiritual father to more than the five that carry his bloodline. Men and women of all walks of life know the name of Howard Miskelly, and to all of them, it speaks of integrity, generosity, kindness, and faith.

As grateful as he is for the honor, though, Howard will tell you that he is not the longest shadow. He will be quick to tell you that his life is nothing more than a testimony to someone who casts the longest shadow of all. And he will gladly open his well-worn, marked-up Bible, turn the thin and wispy pages to the 91st Psalm, and he will read with you the words of the One under whose shadow he gladly falls. And there, in those words, Howard will read to you what he knows is the real story of his life:

The one who lives under the protection of the Most High dwells in the shadow of the Almighty. I will say to the Lord, "My refuge and my fortress, my God, in whom I trust." He Himself will deliver you from the hunter's net, from the destructive plague. He will cover you with His feathers; you will take refuge under His wings. His faithfulness will be a protective shield. You will not fear the terror of the night, the arrow that flies by day, the plague that stalks in darkness, or the pestilence that ravages at noon. Though a thousand fall at your side and ten thousand at your right hand, the pestilence will not reach you. You will only see it with your eyes and witness the punishment of the wicked. Because you have made the Lord-my refuge, the Most High-your dwelling place, no harm will come to you; no plague will come near your tent. For He will give His angels orders concerning you, to protect you in all your ways. They will support you with their hands so that you will not strike your foot against a stone. You will tread on the lion and the cobra; you will trample the young lion and the serpent. Because he is lovingly devoted to Me, I will deliver him; I will exalt him because he knows My name. When he calls out to Me, I will answer him; I will be with him in trouble. I will rescue him and give him honor. I will satisfy him with a long life and show him My salvation.

Endnotes

1. Infantry Journal of the 102nd Division, p. 20-21
2. Ibid, p. 34
3. Ibid, p. 36
4. Ibid, p. 40
5. Ibid, p. 56
6. Ibid, p. 56
7. Ibid, p. 60
8. Ibid, p. 64
9. Ibid., p. 94-95
10. Ibid, p. 101
11. Ibid., p. 158
12. Ibid, p. 163
13. Ibid, p. 163
14. Ibid, p. 163
15. Ibid, p. 164
16. Ibid, p. 167
17. Ibid, p. 167

www.ingramcontent.com/pod-product-compliance
Lightning Source LLC
Chambersburg PA
CBHW022009090426
42741CB00007B/956

* 9 7 8 0 9 9 1 5 7 9 8 3 9 *